Dennis Goodman
Illustrated by Sean Perdue
and Designed by Alan Knight

RuleGraphics by Dennis Goodman
Illustrated by Sean Perdue
Designed by Alan Knight

Printed in the United States of America

First Printing, 2016

ISBN 978-0-9961105-2-5

Library of Congress Control Number: 2016900111

Quantity sales. Special discounts are available on quantity purchases by corporations, associations, and others. For details, inquire at www.betterrulebook.com.

Second Edition

For Kara, Evan and Alex.
- DG

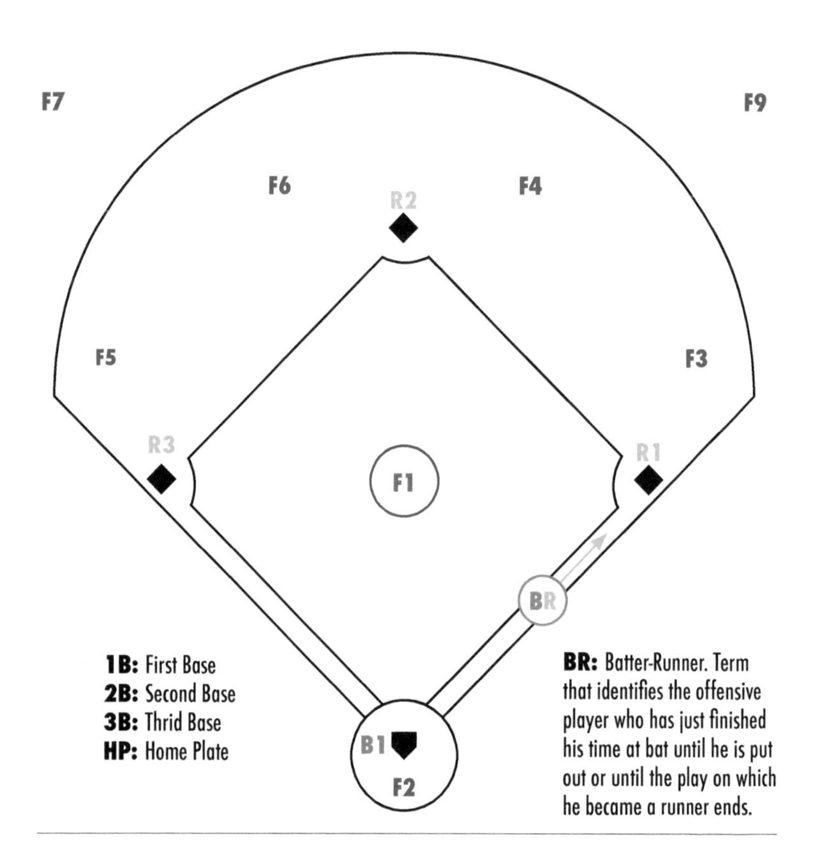

To save space, shorthand is used to describe action in key points and sample plays. The above graphic serves as a key. Similar notation is used in other umpire manuals.

An example is as follows:

Sample Play Written in Shorthand:

R1, R2, 1 out. B1 hits a ground ball to F6 that will be an easy double play. R2 slows up and lets the ball hit him.

If judged to be willful and deliberate interference, the umpire will call R2 and the BR out and return R1 to 1B.

Sample Play Written Normally:

Runners on first and second with one out. The batter hits a ground ball to the shortstop that will be an easy double play. The runner from second slows up and lets the ball hit him.

If judged to be willful and deliberate interference, the umpire will call the runner from second and the batter-runner out and return the runner from first to first base.

Contents

6 Introduction / Notes
8 Scoring a Run
9 Advancing and Touching Bases
10 Foul Tip
11 Uniforms
12 Glove Specification
13 Bats
14 Called or Suspended Game
15 Forfeits
16 Substituting
18 The Windup Position (Pitcher)
19 The Set Position (Pitcher)
20 Strike Zone
21 Balk – Basic Definition
22 Step Balk
23 Other Balks
24 Pitcher Going to his Mouth
25 Substituting for the Pitcher
26 Pitcher/Manager Visits
28 Catch
29 Tag Plays (Base and Player)
30 Force Play
31 Infield Fly Rule
32 Infielder Intentionally Dropping Batted Ball
33 Detached Player Equipment
34 Appeal Plays
36 Batting Out of Order
37 Fair/Foul Ball
38 Batter's Box
39 Batted Ball Hits Batter
40 Bat Infractions around HP
41 Hit by Pitch
42 Batter Interference with Catcher
43 Catcher's Interference
44 Overrunning First Base
45 Runner's Lane Interference
46 Uncaught Third Strike
47 Designated Hitter
49 Two Runners Occupying a Base
50 Passing Another Runner on the Bases
51 Retouching Bases When Ball is Dead
52 Runner Out of Baseline
53 Abandoning Base Paths
54 Runner/Umpire Hit by Batted Ball
55 Interference with Fielder Fielding Batted Ball
56 Willful Interference
57 Placing Runners After Offensive Interference
58 Physically Assisting a Base Runner
59 HP Collisions
60 Ball Thrown Out of Play
61 Ball Lodged in Player or Umpire Equipment
62 Ball Deflected Out of Play
63 Type 1 Obstruction
64 Type 2 Obstruction
65 Spectator Interference
66 Umpire Interference
67 Rule Index
69 OBR Cross Reference
71 Major High School Rule Differences
78 Major College Rule Differences
84 Acknowledgements
85 Biographies

 General  Pitcher  Defense  Batter  Runner

The back of the book contains tables highlighting major rule differences.

An orange box located on top of rule indicates high school rule differs.

 A purple box means the same for the college rule.

Introduction

Hall of Fame manager Leo Durocher once famously said "Baseball is like church. Many attend, few understand". He probably wasn't discussing the rules of the game, but the adage certainly applies to them.

Baseball has hundreds of rule myths and misunderstandings. The number is surprisingly large in light of baseball's revered status as the national pastime.

Fans in any ballpark can be heard spouting "wisdom" passed down through the ages:

- Hands are part of the bat
- That runner touched first base and turned left, so he is out if tagged
- The ball bounced before it hit the batter so he won't be awarded first base
- Batter hit the ball off home plate so it is a foul ball
- Coach high-fived the player so the player is out

None of these are true. So why are these myths so hard to kill?

The answer is the rulebook itself. It is a dense, word heavy slog of a read – a necessity due to the unique nuances of the game. Although it's organized as well as it can be, looking up a specific rule often leads to frustration.

Definitions, situations, penalties and awards for the same play often appear in different sections of the book. Knowing where to look and how to cross reference each section takes time and practice.

Data analysis experts faced a similar challenge: organizing large amounts of complex and confusing data into one coherent story. To combat this problem, they developed a new tool – the infographic – which takes the most important insights and presents them in a simple, visually appealing way.

Infographics and data visualization fundamentally changed the way people digest information. If these infographics can solve the problem in data, why can't they be used for baseball rules?

Ultimately, that's the question that inspired this book. Each RuleGraphic contains the verbatim definition of the rule, key points, sample plays and – where appropriate – a sample picture.
The book is organized by topic and the topics are organized by parts of the game.

Situations are easy to find and all the information needed for basic understanding is located in the graphic. Users know exactly where to look in the rule book to gain deeper knowledge.

This book is not a rulebook substitute; it's a quick, user-friendly reference that makes learning the rules easier. For everyone from aspiring umpires to casual fans, the graphics quickly enable a solid knowledge base.

Reading this won't completely prepare fans to be umpires, but it will make them more informed than the vast majority of other fans. That alone makes the game more fun to watch.

Notes

The book is a primer and reference for Major League Baseball Rules (aka Official Baseball Rules or OBR).

It is not designed to be a substitute for the actual rulebook. The rules are freely available online and used with permission of the Office of the Commissioner of Major League Baseball. The author is not affiliated with Major League Baseball or its umpires.

The tables listing major differences between OBR, high school (NFHS™) and college (NCAA™) rules are intended for reference only. Seek out their individual books for a complete listing of their rules. The author is not affiliated with either organization. Citations are included for easy reference.

Many amateur organizations use the OBR as their base rule set. Those organizations also make modifications to the rules when applicable. Always check the specific organization rulebook for final rulings and interpretations.

Local leagues and tournaments will also modify rules as they see fit. In general, when different, local rulings will supersede the interpretations discussed in this book. Check your local listings.

As in the OBR, any reference in this book to "he," "him" or "his" shall be deemed to be a reference to "she," "her" or "hers," as the case may be, when the person is a female.

The 2015 OBR were used while writing this book. In 2015, Major League Baseball changed the numbering system of their rules. Every effort was made to correctly identify the new rule numbers. There are instances where text of the OBR referred to rules that I could not find in the book. In these instances, I substituted in the rule number I felt MLB was trying to reference. Assume any mistake made in translating was mine.

Any updates or modifications can be found at **www.betterrulebook.com**. If you spot something that is off, please email **dennis@betterrulebook.com**.

General

Rule 5.08:
Scoring a Run

(a) One run shall be scored each time a runner legally advances to and touches first, second, third and home base before three men are put out to end the inning.

EXCEPTION: A run is not scored if the runner advances to home base during a play in which the third out is made.

(1) by the batter-runner before he touches first base;

(2) by any runner being forced out; or

(3) by a preceding runner who is declared out because he failed to touch one of the bases.

(b) When the winning run is scored in the last half-inning of a regulation game, or in the last half of an extra inning, as the result of a base on balls, hit batter or any other play with the bases full which forces the runner on third to advance, the umpire shall not declare the game ended until the runner forced to advance from third has touched home base and the batter-runner has touched first base.

Key Points:

- To score, any runner has to touch HP before the third out is recorded in the inning.
- Even when the run would end the game, runners have a responsibility to touch all their bases. (If the run scores because of an award, only the BR and R3 need advance to the next base.) 5.09(b)(2)(See Page #53) covers abandoning efforts to advance.
- If an appeal (See Page #34) is upheld that causes a runner who is forced or the BR before first to be out, all runs that scored on the play before the appeal do not count.
- If an appeal (See Page #34) is upheld, then any runners behind the runner who is the third out cannot score.
- Once a runner legally scores, he cannot "undo" his run by retouching the plate and retreating toward third.

Sample Plays:

- R1, R3, 1 out. Fly ball hit to F9. R3 tags and heads home, but R1 thinks there are two outs and rounds 2B. After R3 scores, the ball is thrown to 1B to retire R1 for the third out.
  The run counts. R1's third out is not the result of a force out and R3 scored before the out occurred.
- R3, 2 outs. B1 hits a double but misses 1B. R3 easily scores. The defense successfully appeals the BR's miss.
  The BR's out was the third out and it happened before he (legally) touched 1B. The run will not count.
- Bases loaded, 2 outs, Bottom of the 9th inning. B1 hits a single. R1 seeing the hit mobs the batter but never touches 2B. The defense gets the ball and touches 2B.
  Runner at 2B is the third out on a force out. No runs are allowed to score.

Rules 5.06(b)(1), 5.06(b)(4)(I) Comment, and 5.09(c)(2):

Advancing and Touching Bases

5.06(b)(1)

In advancing, a runner shall touch first, second, third and home base in order. If forced to return, he shall retouch all bases in reverse order, unless the ball is dead under any provision of Rule 5.06(c)(5). In such cases, the runner may go directly to his original base.

5.06(b)(4)(I) Comment

The fact a runner is awarded a base or bases without liability to be put out does not relieve him of the responsibility to touch the base he is awarded and all intervening bases. For example: batter hits a ground ball which an infielder throws into the stands but the batter runner missed first base. He may be called out on appeal for missing first base after the ball is put in play even though he was "awarded" second base.

If a runner is forced to return to a base after a catch, he must retouch his original base even though, because of some ground rule or other rule, he is awarded additional bases. He may retouch while the ball is dead and the award is then made from his original base.

5.09(c)(2)

Any runner shall be called out, on appeal, when –

(2) With the ball in play, while advancing or returning to a base, he fails to touch each base in order before he, or a missed base, is tagged.

APPROVED RULING: (A) No runner may return to touch a missed base after a following runner has scored. (B) When the ball is dead, no runner may return to touch a missed base or one he has left after he has advanced to and touched a base beyond the missed base.

Sample Plays:

- R1. B1 hits a ball to deep left field. F7 catches the ball as R1 is on the 3B side of 2B. In returning to 1B, R1 does not retouch 2B.
  R1 would be out on appeal.

- R1. B1 hits a ball to deep left field. F7 catches the ball as R1 is on the 3B side of 2B. In returning to 1B, R1 does not retouch 2B. F7's throw to first goes out of play and R1 is awarded 3B. R1 retouches 1B, touches 2B and proceeds to 3B.
  R1 has corrected his miss of 2B and will not be called out on appeal. This is known as the "last time by" principle.

- B1 hits a homerun but misses 1B. Before he reaches 2B, the coach tells him of his mistake. He turns around and touches 1B.
  This is legal as long as he has not advanced to and touched the base beyond a missed base during the dead ball.

- Bases loaded. B1 hits a ball into the right field gap. R3 misses HP. R2 comes in behind him and touches HP. R3 now goes back and touches the base.
  R3 would be out on appeal. A runner cannot legally return to touch a base after a following runner scores.

Definitions of Terms - FOUL TIP:

Foul Tip

A FOUL TIP is a batted ball that goes sharp and direct from the bat to the catcher's hands and is legally caught. It is not a foul tip unless caught and any foul tip that is caught is a strike, and the ball is in play. It is not a catch if it is a rebound, unless the ball has first touched the catcher's glove or hand.

Key Points:

- A batted ball that does meet the criteria of a foul tip and lands foul becomes a foul ball.
- A catcher is the only player who can catch a foul tip.
- A pitch that bounces and is then hit can be caught for a foul tip.
- A batted ball which has any discernible arc to it and is caught is a foul fly and an out – whether or not the ball goes above the batter's head (or any other arbitrary measuring point).

Sample Plays:

- With an 0-2 count, B1 hits a ball that first bounces off F2's chest protector and into his glove.
  This is a foul ball. The ball must hit F2's glove or hand first to be a foul tip.
- With an 0-2 count, B1 hits a ball off F2's glove. The ball pops into the air and is secured by F2.
  This is a foul tip. B1 has struck out.
- R1 is stealing on a ball that B1 foul tips into F2's glove. Hearing the contact, R1 heads back to 1B. F2 throws to F3 who tags R1 before R1 reaches 1B.
  R1 is out. The ball remains alive on a foul tip.

Rules 3.03 and 6.02(c)(7):
Uniforms

Below are listed some of the specifications and provisions as it pertains to uniforms –

- Uniforms for each team should be the same for each player
- Minimal six inch high numbers on the back
- Solid undershirts should be the same color and be free of letters and insignias for the pitcher
- Sleeves must not be frayed. Sleeves for different players don't have to the same length but should be approximately the same length for each individual player
- No tape on the jersey
- No golf or track spikes
- No shiny buttons
- No advertisements on the jersey
- Nothing that looks like a baseball can be on the jersey
- Jewelry can be worn if not "distracting"

6.02(c)

The pitcher shall not –

(7) Have on his person, or in his possession, any foreign substance.

Rule 6.02(c)(7) Comment: The pitcher may not attach anything to either hand, any finger or either wrist (e.g., Band-Aid, tape, Super Glue, bracelet, etc.). The umpire shall determine if such attachment is indeed a foreign substance for the purpose of Rule 6.02(c)(7), but in no case may the pitcher be allowed to pitch with such attachment to his hand, finger or wrist.

Key Points:

- Umpire will require the player to wear the proper uniform. Failure to do so could result in ejection.
- No player whose uniform does not conform shall be permitted to participate.

Rules 3.04, 3.05, 3.06, and 3.07:
Glove Specification

OBR defines three different types of gloves per rules 3.04, 3.05, and 3.06 – catcher's mitt, first baseman's glove and all others. They all have different specifications for the measurements that can be used.

3.07

(a) The pitcher's glove may not, exclusive of piping, be white, gray, nor, in the judgment of an umpire, distracting in any manner. No fielder, regardless of position, may use a fielding glove that falls within a PANTONE® color set lighter than the current 14-series.

(b) No pitcher shall attach to his glove any foreign material of a color different from the glove.

(c) The umpire-in-chief shall cause a glove that violates Rules 3.07(a) or 3.07(b) to be removed from the game, either on his own initiative, at the recommendation of another umpire or upon complaint of the opposing manager that the umpire-in-chief agrees has merit.

Key Points:

- There is no penalty for using an illegal glove in OBR. If the glove is discovered, it will be removed from the game. Any play made with the illegal glove stands.
    - Catcher's glove shall be no bigger than 38" in circumference and 15 1/2" from top to bottom.
    - First Baseman's glove shall be no bigger than 12" from top to bottom and 8" wide.
    - All other gloves shall be no bigger than 12" tall and 7 3/4" wide.

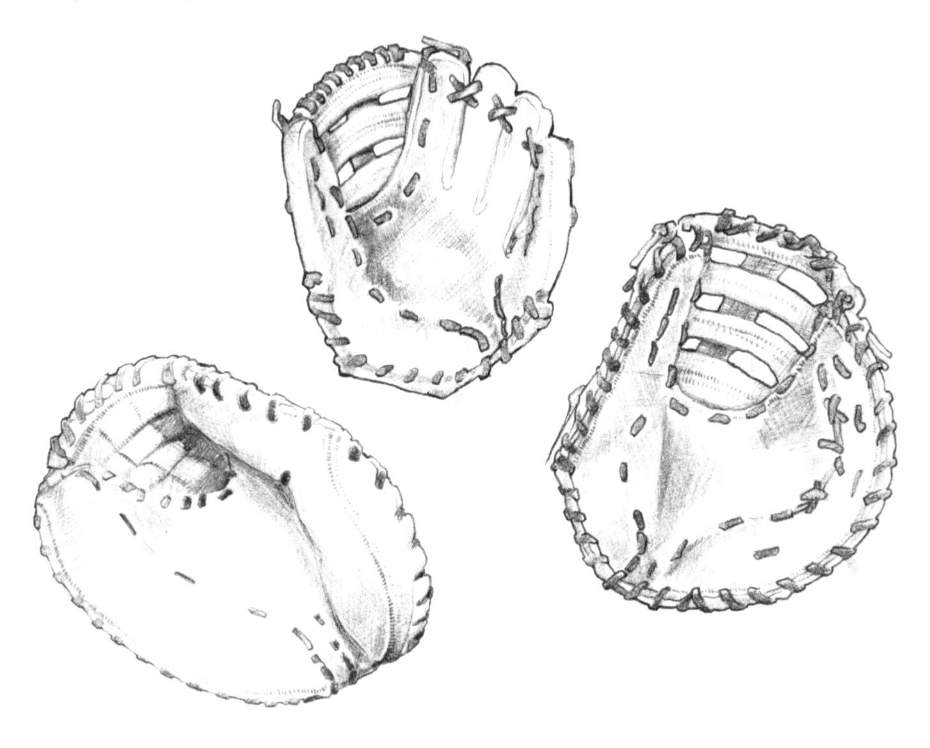

Rules 3.02 and 6.03(a)(4):
Bats

3.02

(a) The bat shall be a smooth, round stick not more than 2.61 inches in diameter at the thickest part and not more than 42 inches in length. The bat shall be one piece of solid wood.

(b) Cupped Bats. An indentation in the end of the bat up to 1 1/4 inches in depth is permitted and may be no wider than two inches and no less than one inch in diameter. The indentation must be curved with no foreign substance added.

(c) The bat handle, for not more than 18 inches from its end, may be covered or treated with any material or substance to improve the grip. Any such material or substance that extends past the 18-inch limitation shall cause the bat to be removed from the game.

(d) No colored bat may be used in a professional game unless approved by the Rules Committee.

6.03(a)

A batter is out for illegal action when –

(4) He uses or attempts to use a bat that, in the umpire's judgment, has been altered or tampered in such a way to improve the distance factor or cause an unusual reaction on the baseball. This includes, bats that are filled, flat-surfaced, nailed, hollowed, grooved or covered with a substance such as paraffin, wax, etc.

No advancement on the bases will be allowed and any out or outs made during a play shall stand.

Key Points:

- For 6.03(a)(4), the illegal bat must be discovered before the next pitch or play to invalidate the action.
- The player is ejected for violating 6.03(a)(4).
- A batter is liable to be called out under 6.03(a)(4) when he enters the batter's box.
- For violation of 3.02, the bat will be removed from the game with no penalty. No out or ejection can come from this rule.

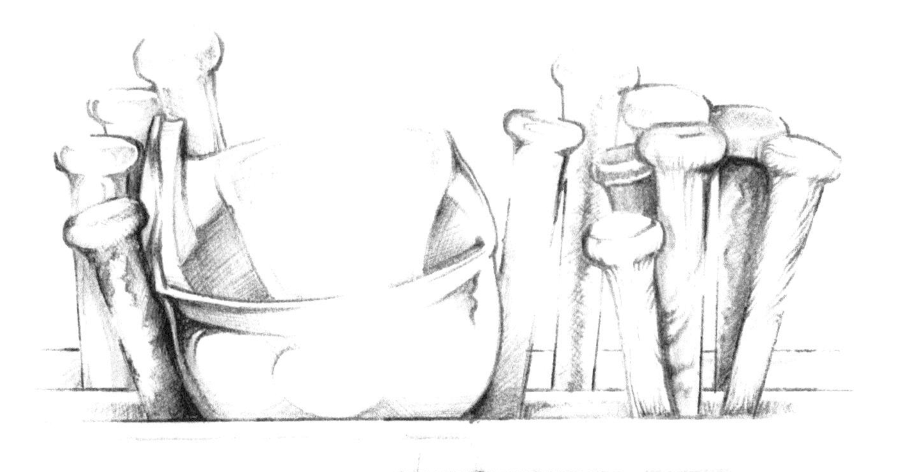

Rules 7.01 and 7.02:
Called or Suspended Game

7.01

(a) A regulation game consists of nine innings, unless extended because of a tie score, or shortened (1) because the home team needs none of its half of the ninth inning or only a fraction of it, or (2) because the umpire-in-chief calls the game.

(b) If the score is tied after nine completed innings play shall continue until (1) the visiting team has scored more total runs than the home team at the end of a completed inning, or (2) the home team scores the winning run in an uncompleted inning.

(c) If a game is called, it is a regulation game:

(1) If five innings have been completed;

(2) If the home team has scored more runs in four or four and a fraction half innings than the visiting team has scored in five completed half-innings;

(3) If the home team scores one or more runs in its half of the fifth inning to tie the score.

(d) If a regulation game is called with the score tied, it shall become a suspended game.

(e) If a game is called before it has become a regulation game, the umpire-in-chief shall declare it "No Game.

7.02

(a) A game shall become a suspended game that must be completed at a future date if the game is terminated for any of the following reasons:

(1) A curfew imposed by law;

(2) A time limit permissible under league rules;

(3) Light failure or malfunction of a mechanical field device under control of the home club. (Mechanical field device shall include automatic tarpaulin or water removal equipment);

(4) Darkness, when a law prevents the lights from being turned on;

(5) Weather, if a regulation game is called while an inning is in progress and before the inning is completed, and the visiting team has scored one or more runs to take the lead, and the home team has not retaken the lead; or

(6) It is a regulation game that is called with the score tied

Key Point:

- Many amateur leagues have their own rules on called or suspended games. Check league rules where applicable.

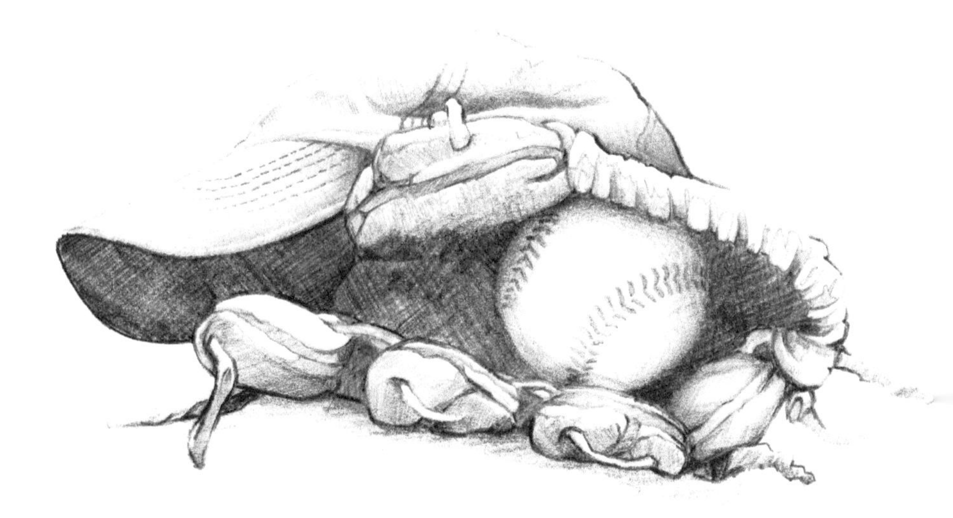

Rule 7.03:
Forfeits

(a) A game may be forfeited to the opposing team when a team –

(1) Fails to appear upon the field, or being upon the field, refuses to start play within five minutes after the umpire-in-chief has called "Play" at the appointed hour for beginning the game, unless such delayed appearance is, in the umpire-in-chief's judgment, unavoidable;

(2) Employs tactics palpably designed to delay or shorten the game;

(3) Refuses to continue play during a game unless the game has been suspended or terminated by the umpire-in-chief;

(4) Fails to resume play, after a suspension, within one minute after the umpire-in chief has called "Play;"

(5) After warning by the umpire, willfully and persistently violates any rules of the game;

(6) Fails to obey within a reasonable time the umpire's order for removal of a player from the game;

(7) Fails to appear for the second game of a doubleheader within twenty minutes after the close of the first game unless the umpire-in-chief of the first game shall have extended the time of the intermission.

(b) A game shall be forfeited to the opposing team when a team is unable or refuses to place nine players on the field.

(c) A game shall be forfeited to the visiting team if, after it has been suspended, the order of the umpire to groundskeepers respecting preparation of the field for resumption of play are not complied with.

Sample Play:

- 1 out, Bottom of the 9th, Score Tied. Team A only has nine players left. B1 is ejected after striking out for the 2nd out.
  The game will continue. If Team A scores, they win. If they don't score, the game is forfeited to Team B.

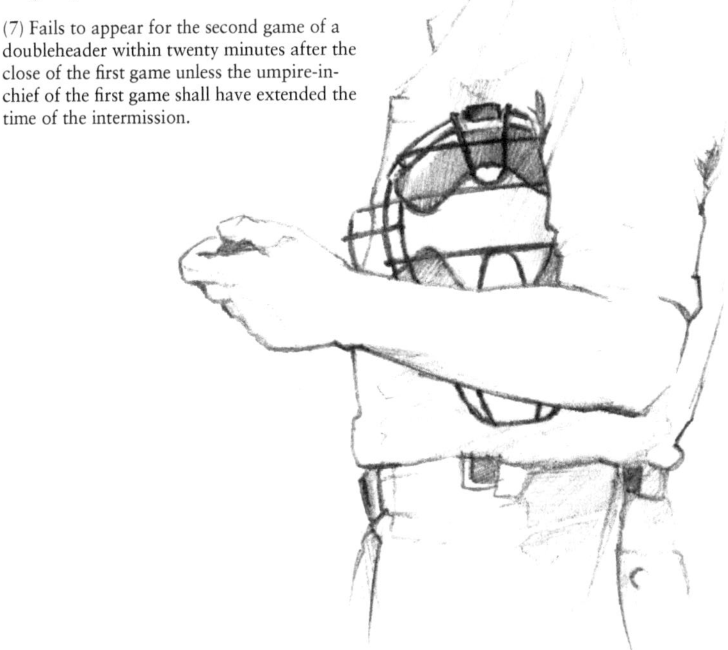

Rule 5.10:
Substituting

(a) A player, or players, may be substituted during a game at any time the ball is dead. A substitute player shall bat in the replaced player's position in the team's batting order.

(d) A player once removed from a game shall not re-enter that game. If a player who has been substituted for attempts to re-enter, or re-enters, the game in any capacity, the umpire-in chief shall direct the player's manager to remove such player from the game immediately upon noticing the player's presence or upon being informed of the player's improper presence by another umpire or by either manager. If such direction to remove the substituted for player occurs before play commences with the substituted-for player improperly in the game, then the substitute player may enter the game. If such direction to remove the substituted- for player occurs after play has commenced with the substituted-for player in the game, then the substitute player shall be deemed to have been removed from the game (in addition to the removal of the substituted-for player) and shall not enter the game. If a substitute enters the game in place of a player-manager, the manager may thereafter go to the coaching lines at his discretion.

Rule 5.10(d) Comment: Any play that occurs while a player appears in a game after having been substituted for shall count. If, in an umpire's judgment, the player re-entered the game knowing that he had been removed, the umpire may eject the manager.

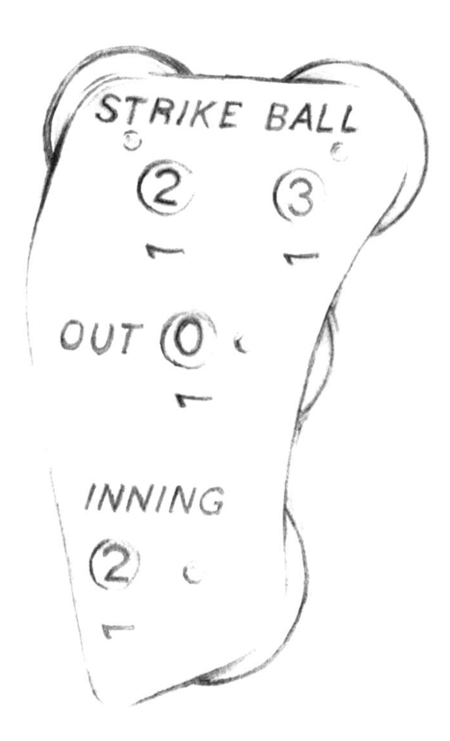

Sample Play:

- Jones who has already left the game illegally re-enters for Smith.
  If play has not started, Smith can come back on the field like he was never substituted for. If play has started, Smith is considered out of the game and a third player must replace Jones.

Key Point:

- Many amateur leagues allow re-entry of players under certain criteria. Check league rules where applicable.

Pitcher

Rule 5.07(a)(1):
The Windup Position (Pitcher)

(1) The Windup Position. The pitcher shall stand facing the batter, his pivot foot in contact with the pitcher's plate and the other foot free. From this position any natural movement associated with his delivery of the ball to the batter commits him to the pitch without interruption or alteration. He shall not raise either foot from the ground, except that in his actual delivery of the ball to the batter, he may take one step backward, and one step forward with his free foot.

When a pitcher holds the ball with both hands in front of his body, with his pivot foot in contact with the pitcher's plate and his other foot free, he will be considered in the Windup Position.

Rule 5.07(a)(1) Comment: In the Windup Position, a pitcher is permitted to have his "free" foot on the rubber, in front of the rubber, behind the rubber or off the side of the rubber.

From the Windup Position, the pitcher may:

(1) deliver the ball to the batter, or
(2) step and throw to a base in an attempt to pick-off a runner, or
(3) disengage the rubber (if he does he must drop his hand to his sides).

In disengaging the rubber the pitcher must step off with his pivot foot and not his free foot first.

He may not go into a set or stretch position—if he does it is a balk.

Key Points:

- The pivot foot is the same foot as the hand a pitcher pitches with (e.g., right foot for right hander).
- The pitcher must step off with the pivot foot by placing it on the ground behind the rubber. If the pitcher "disengages to the front" he has committed a balk.
- If a pitcher steps off correctly, he is now considered an infielder when considering all other rules (especially overthrows).
- It is acceptable for the pitcher to step sideways with his non-pivot foot as part of the windup.
- Pick-off attempts from the windup position are rare, but are legal under OBR as long as he has not made any motion associated with his pitch. Motions associated with his pitch include taking a rocker step with the non-pivot foot, or raising the hands above the head.

Rule 5.07(a)(2):
The Set Position (Pitcher)

(2) The Set Position. Set Position shall be indicated by the pitcher when he stands facing the batter with his pivot foot in contact with, and his other foot in front of, the pitcher's plate, holding the ball in both hands in front of his body and coming to a complete stop. From such Set Position he may deliver the ball to the batter, throw to a base or step backward off the pitcher's plate with his pivot foot.

Before assuming Set Position, the pitcher may elect to make any natural preliminary motion such as that known as "the stretch." But if he so elects, he shall come to Set Position before delivering the ball to the batter. After assuming Set Position, any natural motion associated with his delivery of the ball to the batter commits him to the pitch without alteration or interruption.

Preparatory to coming to a set position, the pitcher shall have one hand on his side; from this position he shall go to his set position as defined in Rule 5.07(a)(2) without interruption and in one continuous motion.

The pitcher, following his stretch, must (a) hold the ball in both hands in front of his body and (b) come to a complete stop. This must be enforced. Umpires should watch this closely. Pitchers are constantly attempting to "beat the rule" in their efforts to hold runners on bases and in cases where the pitcher fails to make a complete "stop" called for in the rules, the umpire should immediately call a "Balk."

Rule 5.07(a)(2) Comment: With no runners on base, the pitcher is not required to come to a complete stop when using the Set Position. If, however, in the umpire's judgment, a pitcher delivers the ball in a deliberate effort to catch the batter off guard, this delivery shall be deemed a quick pitch, for which the penalty is a ball. See Rule 6.02(a)(5) Comment.

Key Points:

- If a pitcher steps off correctly, he is now considered an infielder when considering all other rules (especially overthrows).
- To move from set to windup position, the pitcher must step off the rubber.
- The non-pivot foot must be in front of a line through the front of the rubber, but it does NOT need to be directly in front of (within the 24" width of) the rubber.
- The pitcher must stop before pitching the ball; he does not need to stop before attempting a pick-off. The stop needs to be "complete" but does not need to be "complete and discernable", nor does it need to be for any specific length of time (e.g., one second). To help judge whether the stop was complete, look for the hands to stop moving before the legs begin to move.

Definitions of Terms - *STRIKE ZONE:*
Strike Zone

The STRIKE ZONE is that area over home plate the upper limit of which is a horizontal line at the midpoint between the top of the shoulders and the top of the uniform pants, and the lower level is a line at the hollow beneath the kneecap. The Strike Zone shall be determined from the batter's stance as the batter is prepared to swing at a pitched ball.

Key Points:

- The zone is determined from when the batter is prepared to swing – not from where he is at in his original stance. This is judged from his position after he takes a stride.
- A pitch is ruled a strike if any part of the ball touches any part of the strike zone.

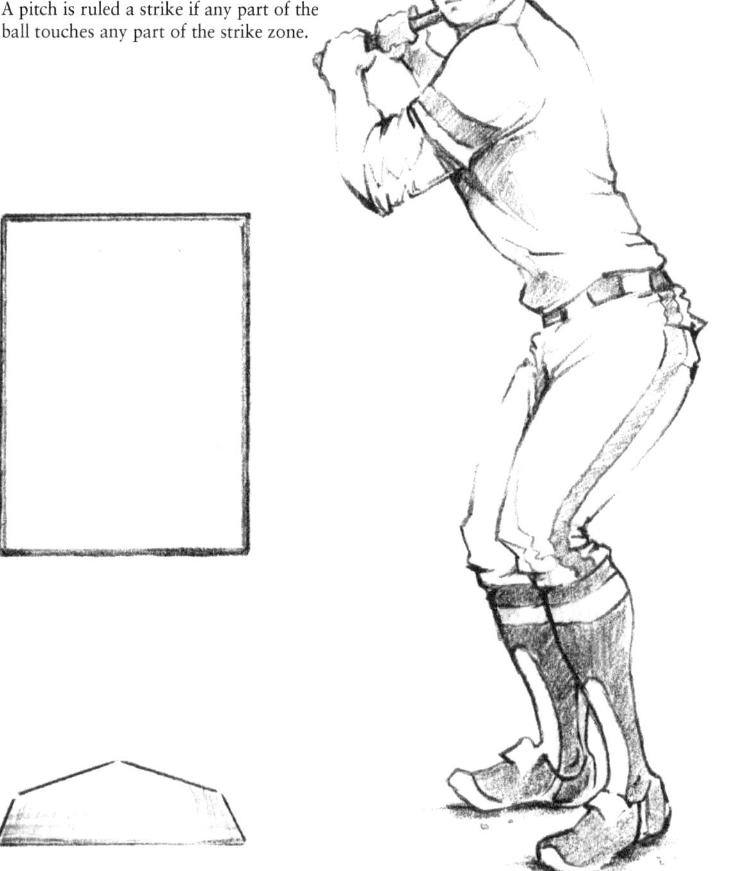

Definitions of Terms - BALK and Rule 6.02(a) PENALTY:

Balk – Basic Definition

A BALK is an illegal act by the pitcher with a runner or runners on base, entitling all runners to advance one base.

6.02(a)

PENALTY: The ball is dead, and each runner shall advance one base without liability to be put out, unless the batter reaches first on a hit, an error, a base on balls, a hit batter, or otherwise, and all other runners advance at least one base, in which case the play proceeds without reference to the balk.

> *APPROVED RULING: In cases where a pitcher balks and throws wild, either to a base or to HP, a runner or runners may advance beyond the base to which he is entitled at his own risk.*

Key Points:

- There are two basic types of balks:

  Illegal Deception - A pitcher knowingly doing something illegal to try and deceive the runner.

  Procedural - Performing an action either specifically outlawed by rule (dropping the ball while on the rubber) or not following correct pitching procedure (switching from the windup position to the set position without disengaging the rubber).

- A balk is a delayed dead ball. If all runners and the batter advance one base then the balk is ignored.

Sample Plays:

- F1 balks and delivers a pitch to B1 who hits a homerun.
  All runners advanced at least one base so the balk is ignored.

- F1 balks and throws wild to 1B. R1 rounds 2B and is thrown out going to 3B.
  R1 advanced one base so the balk is ignored. The out at 3B stands.

- F1 balks and continues with his pitch. B1 swings and misses, but the ball gets past the catcher and rolls to the backstop. R1 misses 2B and is safe at 3B. The defense appeals that R1 missed 2B.
  Even though R1 missed 2B, he is considered to have advanced one base, so the balk is ignored for the runner. The appeal for missing 2B is upheld and R1 is out. The balk is acknowledged for B1 – the swing does not count and he resumes the at bat with the same count as before the pitch.

Rule 6.02(a)(2-3):
Step Balk

If there is a runner, or runners, it is a balk when –

(2) The pitcher, while touching his plate, feints a throw to first or third base and fails to complete the throw;

(3) The pitcher, while touching his plate, fails to step directly toward a base before throwing to that base;

Key Points:

- To be considered stepping towards a base, the angle between his step to 1B or 3B must be 45 degrees or less. An angle greater than 45 degrees means the pitcher is stepping towards HP.
- The step has to happen clearly before the throw. A pitcher cannot "throw ahead of his step."
- This rule is in place when the pitcher is standing on the rubber. When a pitcher is off the rubber, he is treated like any other infielder.
- The rules state the throw has to go to the base – not to the fielder. A throw to a fielder away from the bag who is not breaking to make a play on a runner is a balk.
- When the pitcher lifts his foot toward the "balance point," he is committed to throw to the plate, to 2B or to the base being faced. He cannot throw to the base behind him.
- If the pitcher swings his free foot past the back edge of the rubber, he is required to throw to the plate or to 2B. He cannot throw to 1B or 3B.

Sample Plays:

- R3, R1. F1 steps towards 3B, does not throw, and whirls to throw to 1B.
  Balk - a pitcher cannot feint a throw to 3B.
- R2. F1 spins on his pivot foot and steps towards 2B without throwing.
  Legal – a pitcher can feint towards 2B.
- F1 lifts his foot up and places it down in the same spot while throwing to 1B.
  Balk – a pitcher must gain ground towards a base to be a legal pickoff attempt.

Rule 6.02(a):
Other Balks

Besides a step balk, there are numerous other ways to balk in the rules. These are covered by rule 6.02(a).

Key Points:

- All of the following would result in a balk:
    - o Making a motion associated with the pitch and not delivering the ball.
    - o Throwing to an unoccupied base unless making a play.
    - o Making any motion associated with the pitch while not touching the pitching plate.
    - o Standing astride the rubber without the ball during a "hidden ball trick."
    - o Dropping the ball while on the rubber.
        - If the ball crosses the foul line, it is a ball and not a balk.
    - o Separating the hands without making a pitch or a pickoff attempt. (If the hands are momentarily joined as part of the action of taking the rubber, then the hands are allowed to separate.)
    - o Failing to pitch to the batter (or throw to 2B) when his free foot swings past the back edge of the pitching plate.
    - o Making an Illegal Pitch (a quick return pitch or a pitch while not in contact with the rubber) with runners on base.
        - Without runners on base, the penalty is adding a ball to the count.
    - o Moving from one pitching position to another without legally disengaging the rubber.
- A good rule of thumb is that once a pitcher starts something, he must finish it, with the exception of feinting to 2B. A pitcher cannot start a pitch, and not finish it. He cannot start a pick-off to 1B or 3B and not finish it. He cannot start a pick-off and then pitch.

Sample Play:

- R1 attempts to steal while F1 still has the ball. F1 turns and throws to 2B.
  This is not considered throwing to an unoccupied base since F1 is making a play.

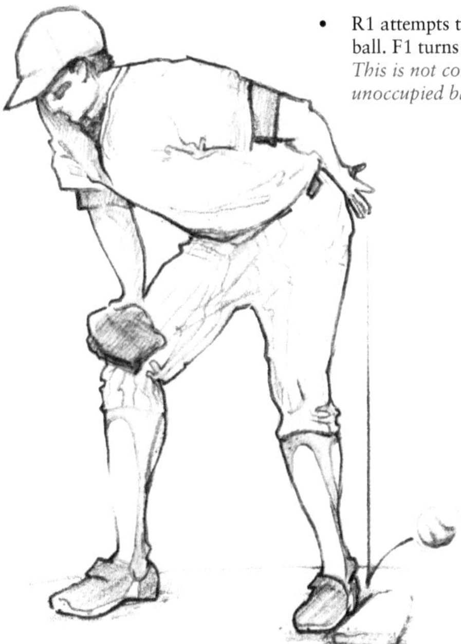

Rule 6.02(c)(1):
Pitcher Going to his Mouth

The pitcher shall not –

> (1) While in the 18-foot circle surrounding the pitcher's plate, touch the ball after touching his mouth or lips, or touch his mouth or lips while he is in contact with the pitcher's plate. The pitcher must clearly wipe the fingers of his pitching hand dry before touching the ball or the pitcher's plate.

EXCEPTION: Provided it is agreed to by both managers, the umpire prior to the start of a game played in cold weather, may permit the pitcher to blow on his hand.

PENALTY: For violation of this part of this rule the umpires shall immediately remove the ball from play and issue a warning to the pitcher. Any subsequent violation shall be called a ball. However, if the pitch is made and a batter reaches first on a hit, an error, a hit batsman or otherwise, and no other runner is put out before advancing at least one base, the play shall proceed without reference to the violation.

Key Point:

- The penalty for this in OBR is never a balk. A warning is given on the first occurrence (for each pitcher) and then a ball is issued.

Rule 5.10:

Substituting for the Pitcher

(f) The pitcher named in the batting order handed the umpire-in-chief, as provided in Rules 4.03(a) and 4.03(b), shall pitch to the first batter or any substitute batter until such batter is put out or reaches first base, unless the pitcher sustains injury or illness which, in the judgment of the umpire-in-chief, incapacitates him from pitching.

(g) If the pitcher is replaced, the substitute pitcher shall pitch to the batter then at bat, or any substitute batter, until such batter is put out or reaches first base, or until the offensive team is put out, unless the substitute pitcher sustains injury or illness which, in the umpire-in-chief's judgment, incapacitates him for further play as a pitcher.

(h) If an improper substitution is made for the pitcher, the umpire shall direct the proper pitcher to return to the game until the provisions of this rule are fulfilled. If the improper pitcher is permitted to pitch, any play that results is legal. The improper pitcher becomes the proper pitcher as soon as he makes his first pitch to the batter, or as soon as any runner is put out.

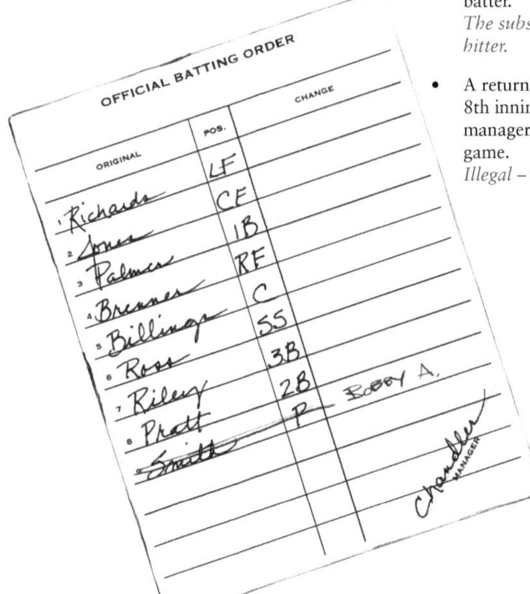

OFFICIAL BATTING ORDER

	ORIGINAL	POS.	CHANGE
1	Richards	LF	
2	Jones	CF	
3	Palmer	1B	
4	Brenner	RF	
5	Billings	C	
6	Ross	SS	
7	Riley	3B	
8	Pratt	2B	
9	~~Smith~~	~~P~~	BOBBY A.

Chandler
MANAGER

(i) If a pitcher who is already in the game crosses the foul line on his way to take his place on the pitcher's plate to start an inning, he shall pitch to the first batter until such batter is put out or reaches first base, unless the batter is substituted for, or the pitcher sustains an injury or illness which, in the judgment of the umpire-in-chief, incapacitates him from pitching. If the pitcher ends the previous inning on base or at bat and does not return to the dugout after the inning is completed, the pitcher is not required to pitch to the first batter of the inning until he makes contact with the pitcher's plate to begin his warm-up pitches.

Key Points:

- The starting pitcher must face one batter.
- A new pitcher must face one batter or retire the side.
- Even though the pitcher must face one batter, the offensive manager can bring out a new hitter at any time.

Sample Plays:

- A substitute replaces F1 in the 8th inning. The offensive coach pinch hits for the next batter.
  The substitute will have to face the pinch hitter.
- A returning pitcher comes out to pitch the 8th inning. After taking his warmups the manager wants to remove him from the game.
  Illegal – the pitcher must face one batter.

Rule 5.10(l):
Pitcher/Manager Visits

A professional league shall adopt the following rule pertaining to the visit of the manager or coach to the pitcher:

(1) This rule limits the number of trips a manager or coach may make to any one pitcher in any one inning;

(2) A second trip to the same pitcher in the same inning will cause this pitcher's automatic removal from the game;

(3) The manager or coach is prohibited from making a second visit to the mound while the same batter is at bat, but

(4) If a pinch-hitter is substituted for this batter, the manager or coach may make a second visit to the mound, but must remove the pitcher from the game.

A manager or coach is considered to have concluded his visit to the mound when he leaves the 18-foot circle surrounding the pitcher's rubber.

Key Points:

- Coaches talking to another player who then talks to the pitcher counts as a visit.
- A coach who makes a second visit to the same pitcher during an at bat will be ejected and the pitcher will be removed when the at bat is over.
- Many amateur organizations do not require the pitcher to be removed from the game. In those organizations, the pitcher is only removed from, and cannot return to, the mound.

Defense

Definitions of Terms - CATCH and Rule 5.09(a)(1): Catch

A CATCH is the act of a fielder in getting secure possession in his hand or glove of a ball in flight and firmly holding it; providing he does not use his cap, protector, pocket or any other part of his uniform in getting possession. It is not a catch, however, if simultaneously or immediately following his contact with the ball, he collides with a player, or with a wall, or if he falls down, and as a result of such collision or falling, drops the ball. It is not a catch if a fielder touches a fly ball which then hits a member of the offensive team or an umpire and then is caught by another defensive player. In establishing the validity of the catch, the fielder shall hold the ball long enough to prove that he has complete control of the ball and that his release of the ball is voluntary and intentional. If the fielder has made the catch and drops the ball while in the act of making a throw following the catch, the ball shall be adjudged to have been caught.

5.09(a)

A batter is out when –

(1) His fair or foul fly ball (other than a foul tip) is legally caught by a fielder;

Rule 5.09(a)(1) Comment: A fielder may reach into, but not step into, a dugout to make a catch, and if he holds the ball, the catch shall be allowed. A fielder, in order to make a catch on a foul ball nearing a dugout or other out-of-play area (such as the stands), must have one or both feet on or over the playing surface (including the lip of the dugout) and neither foot on the ground inside the dugout or in any other out-of-play area. Ball is in play, unless the fielder, after making a legal catch, falls into a dugout or other out-of-play area, in which case the ball is dead.

Key Points:

- The key phrase in the catch definition is "voluntary and intentional" release. A player who gloves a ball, runs six steps, crashes into a wall and drops the ball, has not caught the ball.
- A batted ball can hit off another defensive player and still be caught for an out. A batted ball that hits an umpire or an offensive player cannot be caught for an out.

Sample Plays:

- R1, 1 out. B1 hits the ball to F6. He throws to F4 for a force out. F4 secures the ball and opens his glove to pull the ball out for a throw to complete the double play. The ball drops to the ground.
  R1 is out on the force play. The opening of the glove was a voluntary release. F4 caught the ball and secured an out.
- B1 hits a ball near the dugout. F3 steps into the dugout with one foot on the ground and catches the ball.
  This is not a catch since F3 had a foot on the ground in the dugout. It is a foul ball.
- F9 catches a fly ball for an apparent third out. As F9 is running toward the dugout, he trips over the lip of the infield and inadvertently drops the ball.
  This is still a catch. Once the fielder has demonstrated control of his body and the momentum of making the catch has been completed, the ball is caught.

Definitions of Terms - TAG:
Tag Plays (Base and Player)

A TAG is the action of a fielder in touching a base with his body while holding the ball securely and firmly in his hand or glove; or touching a runner with the ball, or with his hand or glove holding the ball, while holding the ball securely and firmly in his hand or glove. It is not a tag, however, if simultaneously or immediately following his touching a base or touching a runner, the fielder drops the ball. In establishing the validity of the tag, the fielder shall hold the ball long enough to prove that he has complete control of the ball. If the fielder has made a tag and drops the ball while in the act of making a throw following the tag, the tag shall be adjudged to have been made.

Key Points:

- A player must retain control of the ball all the way through the tag and to a voluntary release.
- A fielder can tag a base with any part of his body; a runner must be tagged with the ball (or the glove or hand holding the ball).

Sample Plays:

- With no one on base, B1 hits a sharp grounder to F3. F3 dives and fields the ball. He then rolls on the ground and touches 1B with his throwing hand while controlling the ball.
  The BR is out – this is a legal tag of the base.
- With no one on base, B1 hits a ball to F3. F3 throws to F1 to try and get the out. F1 stumbles after touching 1B and immediately drops the ball.
  The BR is safe. A fielder who drops the ball immediately after tagging a base has not established control.
- R3 is caught in a run-down between 3B and HP. F2 touches R3 with the ball, stumbles and drops the ball.
  R3 is not out.

Definitions of Terms - FORCE PLAY:

Force Play

A FORCE PLAY is a play in which a runner legally loses his right to occupy a base by reason of the batter becoming a runner.

Key Points:

- A runner can only lose his right to the base when the batter becomes a runner. If the BR is retired, runners are no longer forced. However, if a runner misses a base while he is forced, any appeal at that base would be considered a force out, even if the BR is retired before the appeal.
- If two players on a base are tagged, the one who is forced to leave would be called out. (If neither runner is forced, then the trail runner is out.)
- A defensive player can touch a base while in possession of the ball to retire a runner who is forced to run.
- A force is reinstated when a player passes a base while retreating.
- A BR is not forced to first, although it is treated as a force play for all practical purposes.

Sample Plays:

- R1, 1 out. B1 hits a fly ball to F8. F8 throws to F3 before R1 can tag up.
  R1 is out, but this is not a force out. R1 was not forced anywhere because the BR was out.
- R1, 1 out. Ground ball to F3 who touches 1B and then throws to F6 to attempt to retire the runner.
  R1 will have to be tagged out to be retired. Once the BR was retired, no one is forced to any base.
- R1, R2, 1 out. Ground ball to F6 who touches 2B to retire R1.
  R2 is not forced to go to 3B anymore. The BR could take 1B and since R1 is not running to 2B anymore, the force is removed.
- R1. B1 hits a fly ball to F9. R1 rounds 2B but thinks the ball is going to be caught. As he is running back to 1B, the ball drops. F9 throws to F6 who is standing on 2B.
  R1 is out as the force was reinstated.
- R1. B1 hits a grounder to F3. R1 retreats to first. F3 steps on 1B and then tags R1.
  The BR is out, but R1 is safe. The force was removed once F3 touched 1B.
- R1. B1 hits a grounder to F3. R1 retreats to first. F3 tags R1 and then steps on 1B.
  Both R1 and the BR are out.

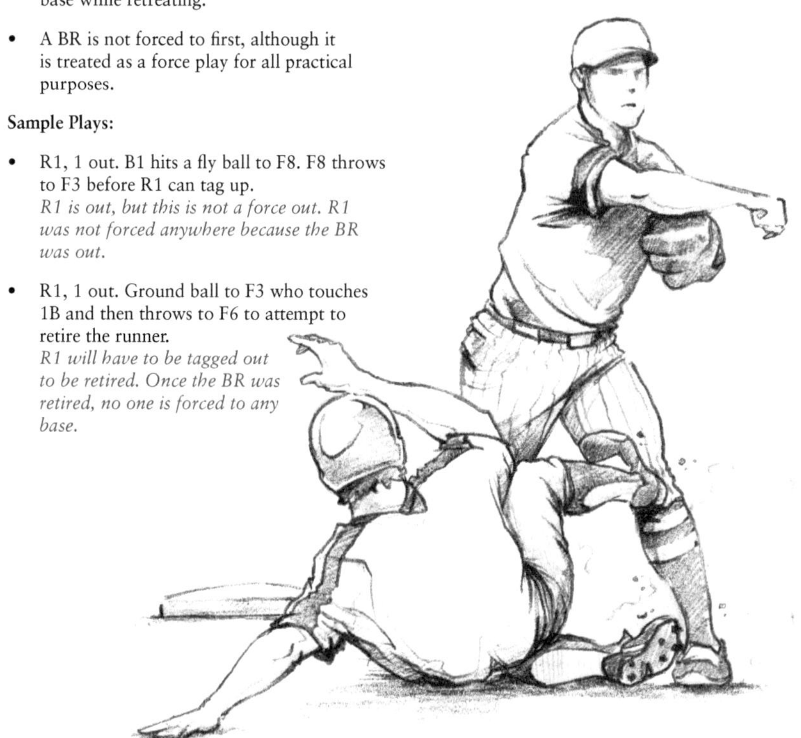

Definitions of Terms - INFIELD FLY:

Infield Fly

An INFIELD FLY is a fair fly ball (not including a line drive nor an attempted bunt) which can be caught by an infielder with ordinary effort, when first and second, or first, second and third bases are occupied, before two are out. The pitcher, catcher and any outfielder who stations himself in the infield on the play shall be considered infielders for the purpose of this rule.

Key Points:

- The batter is out.
- This rule exists to protect the offense. Without this rule, the defense could let the ball drop, pick it up and turn an easy double play. This rule is related to, but separate from, the Intentionally Dropped Ball rule (See Page #32). The ball stays alive in all instances (even an Intentionally Dropped Ball).
- The rule requires that the ball could be caught with ordinary effort by an infielder. Ordinary effort is the effort that a fielder of average skill at a position in that league or classification of leagues should exhibit on a play, with due consideration given to the condition of the field and weather conditions. For example, a fly ball on a calm day could be considered to be an infield fly, while a similar ball hit on a windy day might not be. Sun should not be considered in making this determination. To exhibit ordinary effort, an infielder should be facing the plate and relatively still ("comfortably under the ball").
- An outfielder can end up making the catch – the criteria is that an infielder could have made the catch. Any outfielders who are positioned within the infield at the time of the pitch are considered infielders for the purpose of this rule.
- Remaining runners can advance at their own risk. For these other runners, all provisions of a fly ball apply – if the ball is caught, the runners cannot leave their bases until the ball is touched. If they do so, they are subject to being out on appeal. (Of course, if the ball is not caught, this provision does not apply.) All force outs are removed per rule 5.09(b)(6).

Sample Plays:

- R2, R1, 0 outs. B1 hits a pop-up into shallow left field. F6 is camped out under the ball while touching the grass.
  B1 is out due to the infield fly. The position of the fielder makes no difference in the ruling only the fact it was an infielder. R2 and R1 can advance at their own risk after the catch (if they tagged up) or on a drop.
- Bases loaded, 1 out. B1 hits a pop-up to F5 who lets the ball hit his glove and the ball drops to the ground.
  B1 is out on the infield fly. The ball remains alive and runners can advance at their own risk.
- R2, R1, 1 out. B1 hits a pop-up to F5. At the last minute the sun gets in his eyes and the ball drops. R2 heads towards 3B. F5 grabs the ball and touches the base but not the runner.
  B1 is out on the infield fly. R2 is safe at 3B. Since B1 was out, all force outs were removed. F5 would have to tag R2.
- R2, R1, 0 outs. B1 bunts the ball into the air. F1 lets the ball hit the ground without touching it. F1 throws to F5 to retire R2.
  The bunt means this is not an infield fly. R2 is out on the force out. Note that if F1 touched the ball and let it intentionally drop, B1 would be out due to 5.09(a)(12) and the ball would be dead.

Rule 5.09(a)(12):
Infielder Intentionally Dropping Batted Ball

A batter is out when –

(12) An infielder intentionally drops a fair fly ball or line drive, with first, first and second, first and third, or first, second and third base occupied before two are out. The ball is dead and runner or runners shall return to their original base or bases;

APPROVED RULING: In this situation, the batter is not out if the infielder permits the ball to drop untouched to the ground, except when the Infield Fly rule applies.

Key Points:

- Much like the infield fly, this rule protects the offense from having an easy double play turned against them.
- The ball is not dead if the infield fly is in effect (Definitions of Terms - Infield Fly Comment).

Sample Plays:

- R1, R2, 1 out. B1 hits a sharp line drive to F4. He gloves the ball and then drops it. He throws to 2B for one out and the return throw gets the BR out.
  The ball is dead and B1 is out as soon as F4 drops the ball. R1 and R2 return to the bases occupied at the time of the pitch.
- Bases loaded, 1 out. B1 bunts the ball into the air. In frustration, the BR stands at HP and does not run. F5 lets the ball hit the ground before fielding it. He then throws to F2 who throws to F3 to complete the double play.
  The double play stands. Letting the ball hit the ground is different from intentionally dropping a ball.

Rule 5.06(b)(4)(A-E):
Detached Player Equipment

Each runner including the batter-runner may, without liability to be put out, advance –

(A) To home base, scoring a run, if a fair ball goes out of the playing field in flight and he touched all bases legally; or if a fair ball which, in the umpire's judgment, would have gone out of the playing field in flight, is deflected by the act of a fielder in throwing his glove, cap, or any article of his apparel;

(B) Three bases, if a fielder deliberately touches a fair ball with his cap, mask or any part of his uniform detached from its proper place on his person. The ball is in play and the batter may advance to home base at his peril;

(C) Three bases, if a fielder deliberately throws his glove at and touches a fair ball. The ball is in play and the batter may advance to home base at his peril.

(D) Two bases, if a fielder deliberately touches a thrown ball with his cap, mask or any part of his uniform detached from its proper place on his person. The ball is in play;

(E) Two bases, if a fielder deliberately throws his glove at and touches a thrown ball. The ball is in play;

Key Points:

- If the award is not a homerun, the ball is not dead when a ball is touched by detached equipment and runners can try for more bases.
- Although it's not specifically mentioned in the rules, a pitch is different from a throw – one base is the award for a pitch touched by detached equipment, including the catcher's mask.
- A ball has to be actually touched for the penalty to apply.
- The violation must be intentional. If, for example, a glove comes off during a normal fielding effort and touches the ball, the ball remains alive and in play and no violation has occurred.
- Touching a batted ball over foul territory is a violation only if the ball has a chance to become fair.

Sample Plays:

- B1 hits the ball over F9's head. F9 throws his glove and hits the batted ball. As the ball deflects away, the BR tries to advance to HP and is thrown out.
  The BR is out at HP. The award only covered the BR to 3B. All other advances were at his own risk.
- R2. F2 blocks a pitch in the dirt and scoops it up in his facemask.
  This is touching a pitch with detached equipment. R2 is awarded 3B.
- B1 hits a fly ball to F6. As he shields his eyes from the sun, he accidentally knocks off his cap, which falls into his glove. F6 catches the ball in his cap in his glove.
  B1 is out on the caught fly. The touching with the detached equipment was accidental.

Rule 5.09(c):
Appeal Plays

Any runner shall be called out, on appeal, when –

(1) After a fly ball is caught, he fails to retouch his original base before he or his original base is tagged;

(2) With the ball in play, while advancing or returning to a base, he fails to touch each base in order before he, or a missed base, is tagged.

APPROVED RULING: (A) No runner may return to touch a missed base after a following runner has scored. (B) When the ball is dead, no runner may return to touch a missed base or one he has left after he has advanced to and touched a base beyond the missed base.

(3) He overruns or overslides first base and fails to return to the base immediately, and he or the base is tagged;

(4) He fails to touch home base and makes no attempt to return to that base, and home base is tagged.

Any appeal under this rule must be made before the next pitch, or any play or attempted play. If the violation occurs during a play which ends a half-inning, the appeal must be made before the defensive team leaves the field.

Key Points:

- The ball must be alive for the defense to appeal.
- If the team "errs" (throws the ball out of play or balks) on the appeal – they lose the right to appeal.
- An appeal by itself is not a play (for the purposes of this rule only) meaning multiple appeals can happen after action stops.
- Appeals can sometimes lead to 4th outs. The defense is allowed to take these outs if it is to their advantage.
- There are no accidental appeals. In other words, either the appeal has to be clear or the player has to verbally tell the umpire what he is appealing.
- An appeal for a runner leaving a base too soon on a caught fly ball is not a Force Out (See Page #30). This distinction could affect whether a run counts.
- The defense is considered to have left the field when the pitcher and all infielders have left fair territory.

Sample Plays:

- B1 grounds to F6. F6's throw to F3 goes into the stands. The BR misses 1B and heads to 2B.
  Upon proper appeal, the BR would be out.
- Bases loaded, 1 out. Line drive is caught by F8. Both R3 and R2 leave their bases before F8 touches the ball. F8 lobs the ball to F6 retiring R2, but R3 scores before the third out occurred.
  The defense can appeal R3 leaving early as long as they do so before all infielders have left fair territory. If they appeal, this "4th out" will be taken as it takes a run off the board.
- Bases loaded, 1 out. Line drive is caught by F8. R3 properly tags up, but R2 leaves second before F8 touches the ball. F8 lobs the ball to F6 retiring R2, but R3 scores before the third out occurred.
  R3's run counts. R2 is out on appeal for the third out.
- Bases loaded, 2 outs. B1 hits a base clearing double. R1 misses 2B.
  R1 will be out if appealed. Since R1's out was a force out, no runs score.
- R2, R1. B1 hits a triple. R2 misses 3B on his way home. R1 scores. After R1 scores, R2 goes back and retouches 3B.
  R2 would be out after appeal. A runner cannot legally return to touch a missed base after a following runner scores.

Batter

Rule 6.03(b)(1-3):
Batting Out of Order

(1) A batter shall be called out, on appeal, when he fails to bat in his proper turn, and another batter completes a time at bat in his place.

(2) The proper batter may take his place in the batter's box at any time before the improper batter becomes a runner or is put out, and any balls and strikes shall be counted in the proper batter's time at bat.

(3) When an improper batter becomes a runner or is put out, and the defensive team appeals to the umpire before the first pitch to the next batter of either team, or before any play or attempted play, the umpire shall (1) declare the proper batter out; and (2) nullify any advance or score made because of a ball batted by the improper batter or because of the improper batter's advance to first base on a hit, an error, a base on balls, a hit batter or otherwise

Key Points:

- The batter who was supposed to bat is out – not the batter who actually did bat.
- The umpire should never bring Batting Out of Order to either team's attention.
- If either team notices the wrong batter during the at bat, the proper batter takes his place and assumes the count (with no further penalty).
- Once the at bat has ended, only the defensive team can appeal batting out of order. They must do so before the next pitch or play. If the defensive team properly appeals batting out of order, the player who was supposed to bat is out, all runners return to the base occupied at the time of the pitch, and any outs made on the play are nullified.
- If the defensive team does not appeal, the batter listed directly after the batter who just completed his turn at bat is the proper next batter.

Sample Plays:

Lineup is Able, Baker, Charley, Daniels, Edward.

- Charley comes to the plate and receives one ball. Offensive coach realizes that Baker should be up.
  Baker is placed in the box with a count of 1-0.
- With 1 out, Charley bats improperly for Baker and hits a double. Defense appeals before the next pitch.
  Baker is ruled out for failing to bat in proper order. Charley is now the proper batter and will step into the batter's box again.
- Charley bats improperly for Baker and hits a single. Daniels comes to bat and receives ball 1.
  Once a pitch is thrown to Daniels, Charley's improper at bat becomes proper. Daniels follows Charley on the lineup card and is the proper batter.
- With Able on 1B, Charley bats improperly for Baker and hits a double. Able moves to 3B. The manager appeals that Charley batted out of order.
  The umpire will rule Baker out, put Able back on 1B and Charley will bat again. Note: If Able would have advanced during Charley's at bat via passed ball, steal, wild pitch or balk, that advance would be sustained as it was not a result of the at bat.
- With Able on 1B, Charley bats and hits into a double play. The manager appeals that Charley batted out of order
  Baker is called out, Able is placed back at 1B and Charley bats again.

Definitions of Terms - FAIR AND FOUL BALL:

Fair/Foul Ball

A FAIR BALL is a batted ball that settles on fair ground between home and first base, or between home and third base, or that is on or over fair territory when bounding to the outfield past first or third base, or that touches first, second or third base, or that first falls on fair territory on or beyond first base or third base, or that, while on or over fair territory touches the person of an umpire or player, or that, while over fair territory, passes out of the playing field in flight.

A fair fly shall be judged according to the relative position of the ball and the foul line, including the foul pole, and not as to whether the fielder is on fair or foul territory at the time he touches the ball.

Key Points:

- A foul ball is basically any ball that is not fair.
- If a ball hits any object foreign to the ground in foul territory (Definitions of Terms - Foul Ball), it becomes immediately foul. If it does this in fair territory, it is not fair unless it meets another requirement of a fair ball.
- To meet the requirement of "falls on fair territory on or beyond 1B or 3B" the ball must hit the ground or touch an object beyond the infield square.
- Home Plate is in fair territory.

Sample Plays:

- A ball hits the pitching rubber or a dropped bat in fair territory but then rolls foul before reaching 1B or 3B.
  This is a foul ball.
- A ball hits a dropped bat in foul territory and rolls fair.
  This was a foul ball as soon as it struck the bat.
- A ball bounces over the corner of 3B and lands in foul territory beyond the base.
  This is a fair ball.
- A player whose body is in fair territory reaches over the foul line to touch a ball that is over foul territory.
  This is a foul ball. The location of the ball is what matters, not the location of the player.
- A batted ball with backspin hits in front of HP and spins back into foul territory.
  As long as the ball did not pass 1B or 3B and was not touched, this is a foul ball.

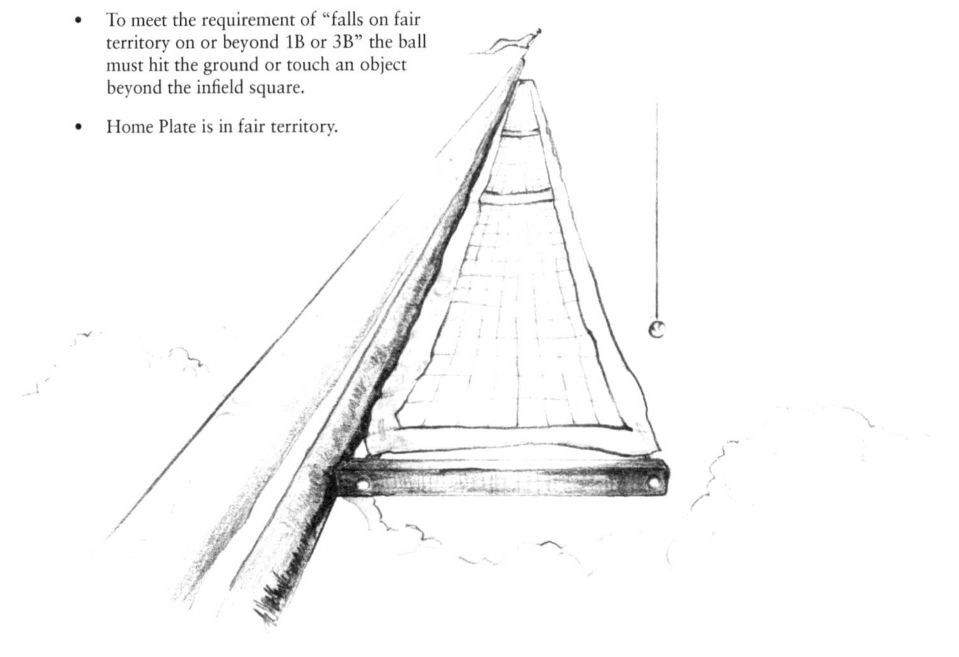

Rules 5.04(b)(5) and 6.03(a)(1):
Batter's Box

5.04(b)

(5) The batter's legal position shall be with both feet within the batter's box.

APPROVED RULING: The lines defining the box are within the batter's box.

6.03(a)

A batter is out for illegal action when—

(1) He hits a ball with one or both feet on the ground entirely outside the batter's box.

Rule 6.03(a)(1) Comment: If a batter hits a ball fair or foul while out of the batter's box, he shall be called out. Umpires should pay particular attention to the position of the batter's feet if he attempts to hit the ball while he is being intentionally passed. A batter cannot jump or step out of the batter's box and hit the ball.

Key Points:

- A batter must start with his feet entirely in the batter's box. This includes his feet touching the line (but not hanging over). If the batter takes his place not in the box, the umpire should direct the player to take a proper stance.
- If the batter strikes the ball (fair or foul) with the entire foot on the ground outside the box when contact is made, the batter is out and the ball is dead.
- A batter's foot can be touching the plate when the batter strikes the ball. As long as the batter's foot is not entirely outside the batter's box, this is legal.

Sample Plays:

- B1 takes his position with the heel of his back foot outside the line of the box.
  Umpire shall instruct B1 to take his position inside the box.
- B1 is fooled on a pitch and hits it with his foot in the air over the ground outside the batter's box.
  Legal as long as contact occurs before B1's foot hits the ground.
- B1 has his foot on the ground outside the batter's box and hits a foul ball.
  B1 is out.
- B1 hits the ball with foot on HP.
  As long as part of his foot is also touching a line of the batter's box, this is legal.

Rules 5.09(a)(7) and 5.04(b)(5):
Batted Ball Hits Batter

5.09(a)

A batter is out when –

> (7) His fair ball touches him before touching a fielder. If the batter is in a legal position in the batter's box, see Rule 5.04(b)(5), and, in the umpire's judgment, there was no intention to interfere with the course of the ball, a batted ball that strikes the batter or his bat shall be ruled a foul ball;

5.04(b)

> (5) The batter's legal position shall be with both feet within the batter's box.
>
> *APPROVED RULING: The lines defining the box are within the batter's box.*

Key Points:

- Both feet have to be on the ground in the box for the batter to be considered in the box.
- The batter's box is partially in fair territory, so a ball could hit the batter in fair territory and it will still be ruled a foul ball.
- The rule is extended to cover so that a ball bouncing off the ground and hitting the bat is also a foul ball if the batter is in the box.
- The ball is dead.

Sample Plays:

- B1 attempts a drag bunt. The batted ball bounces down and hits his foot which is on the ground outside the batter's box
  B1 is out.
- R3. B1 while in the batter's box hits a ball off his shin that rolls to the pitcher. B1 is thrown out at 1B and R3 scores.
  Foul Ball. R3 returns to third and B1 returns to bat.

Rules 5.09(a)(8) and 5.04(b)(5):
Bat Infractions around HP

5.09(a)

A batter is out when –

(8) After hitting or bunting a fair ball, his bat hits the ball a second time in fair territory. The ball is dead and no runners may advance. If the batter-runner drops his bat and the ball rolls against the bat in fair territory and, in the umpire's judgment, there was no intention to interfere with the course of the ball, the ball is alive and in play. If the batter is in a legal position in the batter's box, see Rule 5.04(b)(5), and, in the umpire's judgment, there was no intention to interfere with the course of the ball, a batted ball that strikes the batter or his bat shall be ruled a foul ball;

5.04(b)

(5) The batter's legal position shall be with both feet within the batter's box.

APPROVED RULING: The lines defining the box are within the batter's box.

Key Points:

- There is a distinction between bat hitting ball (batter is out) and ball hitting bat (a live ball).
- If a player throws a bat and it interferes with a fielder in fair or foul territory, the batter is out.
- If a ball hits a broken bat or if a broken bat interferes with a fielder, the ball is alive and no interference is called.
- A batter cannot intentionally deflect a ball over foul territory that has a chance of becoming a fair ball – he is out and the ball is dead via 5.09(a)(9).

Sample Plays:

- B1 throws his bat at an outside pitch. The ball is hit towards F1 who has to dodge the bat to field the ball.
  B1 is out. Note that the out is for interference, not for hitting the pitch with a bat that is no longer in B1's hands.
- After bunting the ball, the BR lays his bat on the ground. The ball rolls against the bat.
  As long as the BR did not intentionally hit the ball or intentionally place the bat in the ball's path, the ball is in play.

Rule 5.05(b)(2):
Hit by Pitch

The batter becomes a runner and is entitled to first base without liability to be put out (provided he advances to and touches first base) when –

(2) He is touched by a pitched ball which he is not attempting to hit unless (A) The ball is in the strike zone when it touches the batter, or (B) The batter makes no attempt to avoid being touched by the ball;

If the ball is in the strike zone when it touches the batter, it shall be called a strike, whether or not the batter tries to avoid the ball. If the ball is outside the strike zone when it touches the batter, it shall be called a ball if he makes no attempt to avoid being touched.

APPROVED RULING: When the batter is touched by a pitched ball which does not entitle him to first base, the ball is dead and no runner may advance.

Key Points:

- The rule does not state "touched by an in-flight ball." A batter hit by a pitch that bounces is considered to be hit by the pitch.
- The hands are considered part of the player's body per rule Definitions of Terms - TOUCH. If the batter is swinging when he gets hit on the hands it is a strike. If the batter is not swinging, it is a hit by pitch.
- The ball is dead per 5.06(c)(1) any time the batter is hit.

Sample Plays:

- R1 is stealing and B1 is batting with a 1-2 count. B1 swings and misses a ball that hits him and R1 reaches 2B
  B1 is charged a strike since he swung per Definitions of Terms - STRIKE(e) and is out. The ball is dead so R1 must return to 1B.
- R2, 0 outs. The pitch strikes B1's hands as he is beginning his swing.
  Ball is dead once it touches B1's hands. If the umpire rules a swing was not attempted, B1 gets 1B; otherwise add a strike to the count.
- 1-1 count and B1 leans his elbow into the strike zone and gets hit by a slow curve ball.
  Ball is dead, a strike is called. The updated count is 1-2.

Rule 6.03(a)(3):
Batter Interference with Catcher

6.03(a)

A batter is out for illegal action when –

(3) He interferes with the catcher's fielding or throwing by stepping out of the batter's box or making any other movement that hinders the catcher's play at home base.

Key Points:

- This is a delayed dead ball. If the runner trying to steal is put out on the initial throw, it is assumed there was no interference and no penalty is imposed. However, if the initial throw does not retire the runner, he is returned to his base and the batter is out.
- Exception: If the runner is coming home AND there are less than two outs, the runner (and not the batter) is out.

Sample Plays:

- R1 is stealing on the play when B1 leans out in front of the catcher interfering with his ability to throw. R1 is safe.
  B1 is called out and R1 is returned to 1B.
- R2 is stealing 3B when B1 interferes with F2. F2 is able to still throw out R2.
  Disregard the interference.
- R3 is running home for a squeeze play. B1 steps across HP blocking F2's attempt to make a tag.
  R3 is out for B1's interference unless there are already two outs – then B1 is out.
- R1 is stealing, B1 takes a hard swing and unintentionally hits F2 on his backswing.
  B1 is not out for interference, and R1 is returned to 1B. The ball is dead.

Rule 5.05(b)(3):
Catcher's Interference

The batter becomes a runner and is entitled to first base without liability to be put out (provided he advances to and touches first base) when –

> (3) The catcher or any fielder interferes with him. If a play follows the interference, the manager of the offense may advise the plate umpire that he elects to decline the interference penalty and accept the play.
>
> Such election shall be made immediately at the end of the play. However, if the batter reaches first base on a hit, an error, a base on balls, a hit batsman, or otherwise, and all other runners advance at least one base, the play proceeds without reference to the interference.

Key Points:

- The batter gets the right to advance to 1B
- If a runner is trying to steal on the play, he is entitled to that base via 5.06(b)(3)(D). Otherwise, other runners only advance if forced
- In addition, if a runner is trying for home on a steal or a squeeze play, then the pitcher is charged with a balk and all runners advance (Rule 6.01(g)), even if they were not attempting to advance at the time of the interference.

Sample Plays:

- Bases empty. B1's bat is touched by F2 on the swing. Ball is popped up and caught.
  B1 is awarded 1B.
- R2 is stealing on the play and B1 is interfered with by F2 and grounds out to 1B.
  B1 is given 1B and R2 is given 3B since he was stealing on the play.
- R3, 1 out. B1 is interfered with by F2 and still hits a fly ball to F9. R3 tags and scores.
  Offensive coach will be given the choice of runners on 1B and 3B and one out (enforce the interference) or bases empty, 2 outs and one run scored (take the play).
- R1 is stealing when B1 is interfered with by F2. B1 grounds a base hit to center field. R1 is thrown out trying to obtain 3B.
  Since both the batter and each runner obtained at least one base, the interference is disregarded. R1 was only protected for one base and his out at 3B stands.

5.09(b)(11):
Overrunning First Base

Any runner is out when –

(11) He fails to return at once to first base after overrunning or oversliding that base. If he attempts to run to second he is out when tagged. If, after overrunning or oversliding first base he starts toward the dugout, or toward his position, and fails to return to first base at once, he is out, on appeal, when he or the base is tagged;

Key Points:

- The runner is out if he "attempts" to run to second. This attempt need not be significant – even a brief stutter-step toward second can indicate an attempt for second.
- The rule does NOT specify which way the runner must turn. If a runner turns left (toward second) but does not attempt, he will not be out if he is tagged.
- Rule 5.09(b)(2) further covers abandoning his efforts to advance.

Sample Plays:

- R3, 2 outs, B1 hits a slow roller to F5. Throw to 1B is wild. The BR touches 1B and makes a slight attempt towards 2B and is tagged. R3 scored before the tag.
  The BR is out. However he reached 1B before being out, so R3's run scores.
- B1 walks and hustles down to 1B. He overruns 1B and is tagged.
  As long as he did not attempt to go to 2B, he is ruled safe.
- B1 hits the ball to F6 who throws to F3 resulting in a close play. The umpire calls the BR safe. He does not realize this, drops his helmet and starts walking toward his position in the outfield.
  Once the BR has progressed a "reasonable distance" (5.09(b)(2) PLAY) still indicating he believes he is out, he will be declared out.

Rule 5.09(a)(11):
Runner's Lane Interference

A batter is out when –

(11) In running the last half of the distance from home base to first base, while the ball is being fielded to first base, he runs outside (to the right of) the three-foot line, or inside (to the left of) the foul line, and in the umpire's judgment in so doing interferes with the fielder taking the throw at first base, in which case the ball is dead; except that he may run outside (to the right of) the three-foot line or inside (to the left of) the foul line to avoid a fielder attempting to field a batted ball;

Rule 5.09(a)(11) Comment: The lines marking the three-foot lane are a part of that lane and a batter-runner is required to have both feet within the three-foot lane or on the lines marking the lane. The batter-runner is permitted to exit the three-foot lane by means of a step, stride, reach or slide in the immediate vicinity of first base for the sole purpose of touching first base.

Key Points:

- Both feet have to be within the lane (or in the air having last touched within the lane) to be legal.
- The lines are considered part of the lane.
- If the runner has been in the lane, he is allowed to leave the lane in his last step to the base.
- A quality throw (one which could reasonably be expected to retire the runner) is required to call the runner out.
- All other runners are placed where they were at time of pitch unless an intervening play occurred at home plate with less than 2 outs where a runner scored (6.01(a) PENALTY).

Sample Plays:

- R2. B1 bunts the ball in front of the HP. While running with one foot outside the running lane, the throw from F2 hits the BR in the back.
  The ball is dead, the BR is out and R2 returns to 2B.
- B1 hits a dribbler to F2. The BR is running outside the running lane as F2 throws the ball over F3's head.
  BR is not out. A quality throw is required to call interference.
- B1 hits a dribbler to F2. F2's throw to 1B hits the BR in fair territory before he has reached the running lane.
  The BR is not out. The running lane restrictions apply only when the BR is more than halfway to 1B.
- Bases loaded. B1 hits a ground ball to F3. F3 throws home in an attempt to retire R3, but the throw hits the BR who is running outside the running lane.
  The play stands and the ball remains alive. The rule covers attempts to retire the BR at 1B.

Rules 5.09(a)(2-3) and 5.05(a)(2):
Uncaught Third Strike

5.09(a)

A batter is out when –

(2) A third strike is legally caught by the catcher;

Rule 5.09(a)(2) Comment: "Legally caught" means in the catcher's glove before the ball touches the ground. It is not legal if the ball lodges in his clothing or paraphernalia; or if it touches the umpire and is caught by the catcher on the rebound.

If a foul tip first strikes the catcher's glove and then goes on through and is caught by both hands against his body or protector, before the ball touches the ground, it is a strike, and if third strike, batter is out. If smothered against his body or protector, it is a catch provided the ball struck the catcher's glove or hand first.

(3) A third strike is not caught by the catcher when first base is occupied before two are out;

5.05(a)

The batter becomes a runner when –

(2) The third strike called by the umpire is not caught, providing (1) first base is unoccupied, or (2) first base is occupied with two out;

Key Points:

- A pitch that touches the ground and then skips into the catcher's glove cannot be caught for a third strike.
- A pitch that touches the ground and is then swung at and foul tipped into the catcher's glove is a caught strike.
- This rule originally allowed all batters to attempt to advance to first after three strikes. It was changed to prevent catchers from dropping the pitch when 1B was occupied to get an easy double play.

Sample Plays:

- R1, 1 out. Runner is stealing on the play. B1 swings and misses a pitch that is not caught.
  B1 is out since 1B was occupied at the time of the pitch with less than two outs.
- Bases loaded, 2 outs. B1 swings at strike 3 with an uncaught pitch. F2 picks up the ball and touches HP.
  R3 is out. B1 became a runner on strike 3 forcing all other runners. F2 retired R3 on a force out.
- B1 swings at an uncaught third strike, does not realize he can run and starts returning to the dugout.
  The BR is officially out once he leaves the dirt circle surrounding HP.

Rule 5.11:

Designated Hitter

(a) The Designated Hitter Rule provides as follows:

(1) A hitter may be designated to bat for the starting pitcher and all subsequent pitchers in any game without otherwise affecting the status of the pitcher(s) in the game. A Designated Hitter for the pitcher, if any, must be selected prior to the game and must be included in the lineup cards presented to the Umpire-in- Chief.

Key Points:

- Any substitute (other than the pitcher) for the DH (at bat or as a runner) becomes the DH.
- If the DH is not provided before the game or is terminated during the game, the pitcher's position is now in the batting lineup for the remainder of the game.
- The DH is terminated under the following circumstances
  - o The DH takes the field
  - o The pitcher bats (can only bat for the DH)
  - o The pitcher takes another position on defense
  - o A pinch hitter for another batter takes the mound
- The DH must bat at least once unless the defense changes pitcher.
- The DH is "locked" into his position in the batting order.
- Many amateur leagues allow a DH for a player other than the pitcher. Check league rules where applicable.

Sample Play:

- In the 8th inning, the DH, who is batting 4th, takes the place of F3, who is batting 7th.
  The DH is terminated for the remainder of the game.The DH remains in the 4th position of the batting order.
  F1 will bat in the 7th position (for F3.)

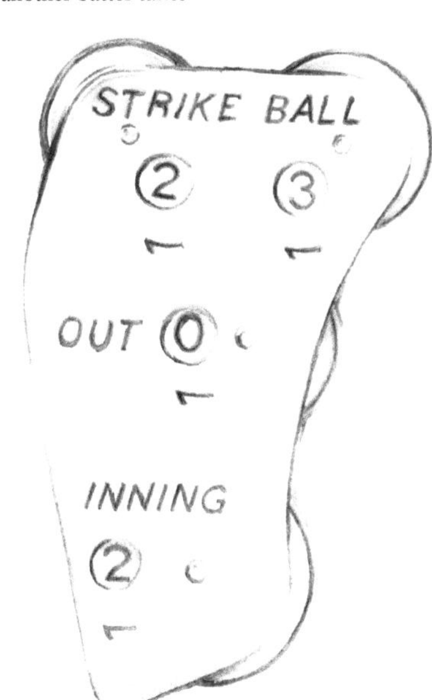

Runner

Rules 5.06(a)(1-2) and 5.06(b)(2):
Two Runners Occupying a Base

5.06(a)

(1) A runner acquires the right to an unoccupied base when he touches it before he is out. He is then entitled to it until he is put out, or forced to vacate it for another runner legally entitled to that base.

(2) Two runners may not occupy a base, but if, while the ball is alive, two runners are touching a base, the following runner shall be out when tagged and the preceding runner is entitled to the base, unless Rule 5.06(b)(2) applies.

5.06(b)

(2) If a runner is forced to advance by reason of the batter becoming a runner and two runners are touching a base to which the following runner is forced, the following runner is entitled to the base and the preceding runner shall be out when tagged or when a fielder possesses the ball and touches the base to which such preceding runner is forced.

Key Points:

- Occupying a base is a different concept from being legally entitled to a base.
- A runner is legally entitled to a base until he is forced from that base or until he reaches the next base. For example, R3 is entitled to 3B until he reaches home or until he is forced from 3B. This is important when runners are returned to their last legally occupied base.

Sample Plays:

- R2, R3, 1 out. B1 hits a blooper to F7. R2 sees it drop and is standing on 3B. R3 never advances and is also standing on 3B. F5 tags both runners.
  R2 is out. R3 is entitled to the base until he leaves or is forced to leave.
- R1, R2, 1 out. A sharp line drive one hops into F6's glove. R2 thinks it is caught and stays on the base. R1 sees it drop and is also standing on 2B. F6 tags both runners.
  R2 is out since he was forced to vacate 2B once B1 became a runner.
- R3 is caught in a run-down between 3B and HP. As the run-down continues, R2 advances and is touching 3B. R3 slaps the ball out of the glove of the catcher.
  R3 is out for interference. R2 is returned to 2B as that was his last legally acquired base at the time of the interference. Even though he reached 3B, it was still R3's base.

Rule 5.09(b)(9):
Passing Another Runner on the Bases

Any runner is out when –

(9) He passes a preceding runner before such runner is out;

Key Points:

- The ball remains alive when this happens.
- A runner is out on this provision even if the ball happens to be dead at the time.
- A runner has to be completely ahead of the runner before considered to have passed (equal is not passing).
- Passing a runner creates a time play with 2 outs.
- If the BR passes R1 during a fly ball that is caught, the caught ball takes precedence over the out for passing a runner.

Sample Plays:

- R1, no outs. B1 hits a sinking line drive to F8. The ball hits the ground. R1 thinks the ball is caught and retreats to 1B and in doing so crosses the BR who rounded 1B. *Even though R1 was the one that created the passing by running behind the BR, the BR is still out for passing the runner. The force play is removed when this happens.*
- Bases loaded, 2 outs. B1 hits a ball into the gap. R1 pulls his hamstring and is hopping between 1B and 2B and is passed by the BR. *The BR is out for the 3rd out. Since this is not a force out and the BR reached 1B, any runs that scored before the passing shall count.*
- Bases loaded, 1 out. B1 hits a ball into the gap. R1 pulls his hamstring and is hopping between 1B and 2B and is passed by the BR. The ball is relayed home to put out R2 at HP. *The BR is out for passing the runner. Since the ball is not dead, the defense has the opportunity to play on other runners. R2's out at the plate stands.*

Rule 5.09(c)(2):
Retouching Bases When Ball is Dead

Any runner shall be called out, on appeal, when –

(2) With the ball in play, while advancing or returning to a base, he fails to touch each base in order before he, or a missed base, is tagged.

APPROVED RULING: (B) When the ball is dead, no runner may return to touch a missed base or one he has left after he has advanced to and touched a base beyond the missed base.

Key Points:

- "Base Beyond" refers to the next base relative to where the runner is when the ball became dead or relative to any base missed after the ball became dead.
- If the runner happens to return to a missed base after advancing and touching a base beyond, he shall be ruled out upon proper appeal.

Sample Plays:

- B1 hits a HR. He misses 1B. Before he reaches 2B, he retreats and touches 1B.
  This is legal.
- R1 is stealing with 1 out. B1 hits a line drive to F6 who throws the ball out of play trying to put out R1. The umpire properly awards R1 3B. After the ball is out of play, R1 advances and touches 2B when his coach reminds R1 to touch 1B. He retreats back, touches 1B and advances to 3B, touching 2B along the way.
  R1 touched a base beyond his position after the ball was dead. He will be called out upon proper appeal.
- R1 is stealing with 1 out. He is around 2B when F9 catches a fly ball. F9 throws the ball out of play. R1 is awarded home. He retreats and touches 1B and completes his award.
  This is legal. Once R1 retouches first, the award is changed to 3B. R1's retouch of 1B would be illegal if he touched 3B after the ball was dead.

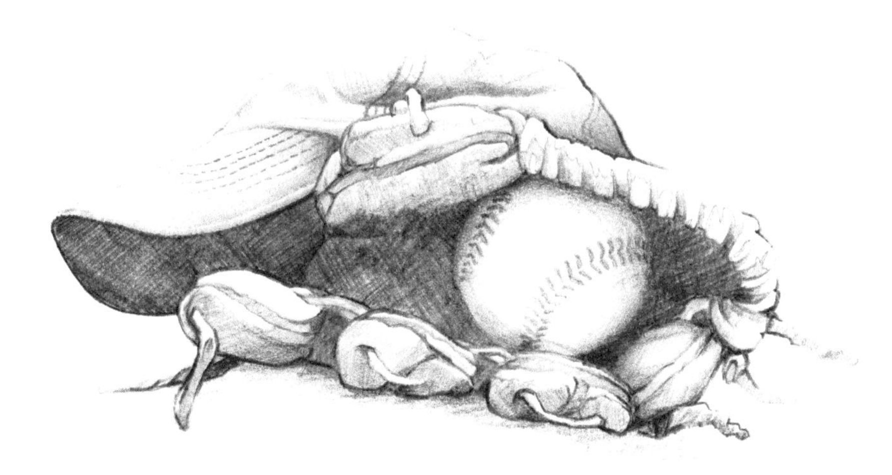

Rule 5.09(b)(1):
Runner Out of Baseline

Any runner is out when –

(1) He runs more than three feet away from his base path to avoid being tagged unless his action is to avoid interference with a fielder fielding a batted ball. A runner's base path is established when the tag attempt occurs and is a straight line from the runner to the base he is attempting to reach safely.

Key Points:

- The runner is only out if he runs out of his base path to avoid being tagged.
- The base path is defined as being a line from the runner to the base – not the actual baseline (a direct line between the bases).

Sample Plays:

- B1 hits a ball into the right center field gap. On his way from 1B to 2B he zig-zags back and forth more than 3 feet outside the baseline.
  Legal – No tag is being attempted.
- B1 strikes out but the pitch hits the dirt. He is three feet from HP before realizing he can run. The catcher attempts a tag.
  His base path is from where he is standing at this point to 1B. Even though he is three feet from HP, he is not out for being out of the baseline unless he moves three feet from his current spot.
- R1 moves 5 feet out of the baseline to avoid F4 who is fielding a ground ball.
  Legal – a runner can be out of the baseline to avoid interfering with a fielder.

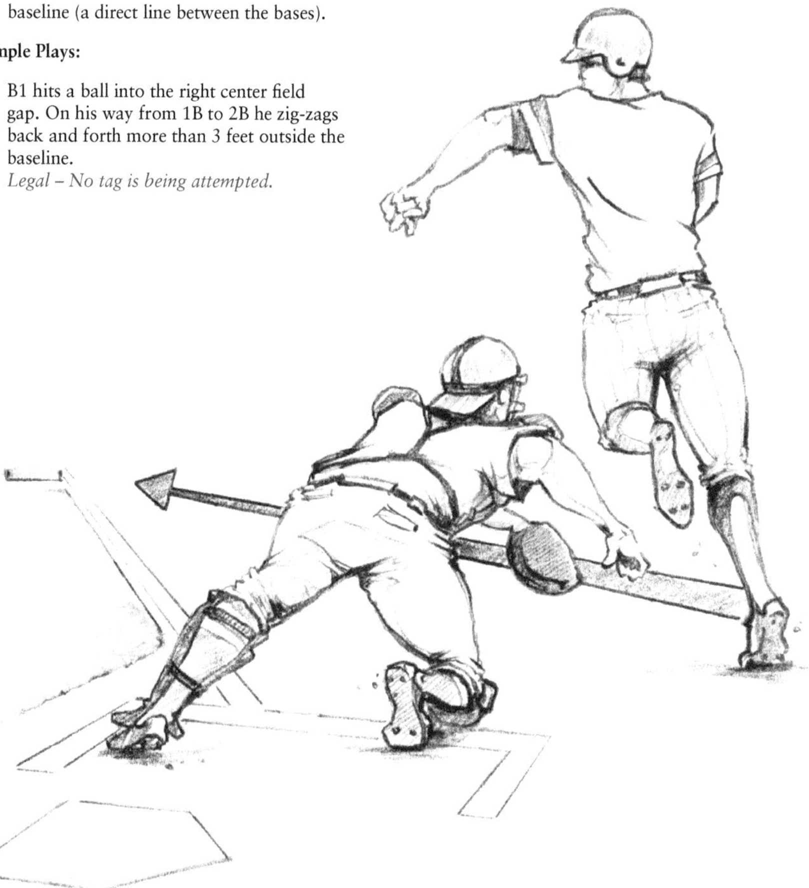

Rule 5.09(b)(2):
Abandoning Base Paths

Any runner is out when –

(2) after touching first base, he leaves the base path, obviously abandoning his effort to touch the next base;

Rule 5.09(b)(2) Comment: Any runner after reaching first base who leaves the base path heading for his dugout or his position believing that there is no further play, may be declared out if the umpire judges the act of the runner to be considered abandoning his efforts to run the bases. Even though an out is called, the ball remains in play in regard to any other runner.

This rule also covers the following and similar plays: Less than two out, score tied last of ninth inning, runner on first, batter hits a ball out of park for winning run, the runner on first passes second and thinking the home run automatically wins the game, cuts across diamond toward his bench as batter-runner circles bases. In this case, the base runner would be called out "for abandoning his effort to touch the next base" and batter-runner permitted to continue around bases to make his home run valid.

If there are two out, home run would not count (see Rule 5.09(d)). This is not an appeal play.

Key Points:

- Abandoning the base paths with two outs leads to a time play (not an appeal play). If the abandoning occurs before the run scores, the run would not count. An out for abandonment is NOT considered a force out (although the defense can appeal the missed base to create a force out).
- Different criteria are used to determine when someone has abandoned his efforts to run versus when someone has given up his opportunity to run after an uncaught third strike (See Page #46).
- When the winning run is forced in as the result of an award with the bases loaded, the game ends when R3 touches HP and the BR touches 1B. If either refuses to advance, the offender is called out and the game resumes.
- When the winning run is forced in as the result of a batted ball with the bases loaded, all runners must advance or be subject to being put out.

Sample Play:

- With 2 outs, B1 hits a ground ball to a diving F6. The throw to F3 is in time but F3 drops the ball. Frustrated with being "out", the BR continues towards his outfield position.
  The BR shall be called out for abandoning his efforts to run the bases.

Rules 5.06(c)(6) and 5.09(b)(7):
Runner/Umpire Hit by Batted Ball

5.06(c)

The ball becomes dead and runners advance one base, or return to their bases, without liability to be put out, when –

(6) A fair ball touches a runner or an umpire on fair territory before it touches an infielder including the pitcher, or touches an umpire before it has passed an infielder other than the pitcher; runners advance, if forced.

If a fair ball goes through, or by, an infielder, no other infielder has a chance to make a play on the ball and the ball touches a runner immediately behind the infielder that the ball went through, or by, the ball is in play and the umpire shall not declare the runner out. If a fair ball touches a runner after being deflected by an infielder, the ball is in play and the umpire shall not declare the runner out;

5.09(b)

Any runner is out when –

(7) He is touched by a fair ball in fair territory before the ball has touched or passed an infielder. The ball is dead and no runner may score, nor runners advance, except runners forced to advance. EXCEPTION: If a runner is touching his base when touched by an Infield Fly, he is not out, although the batter is out;

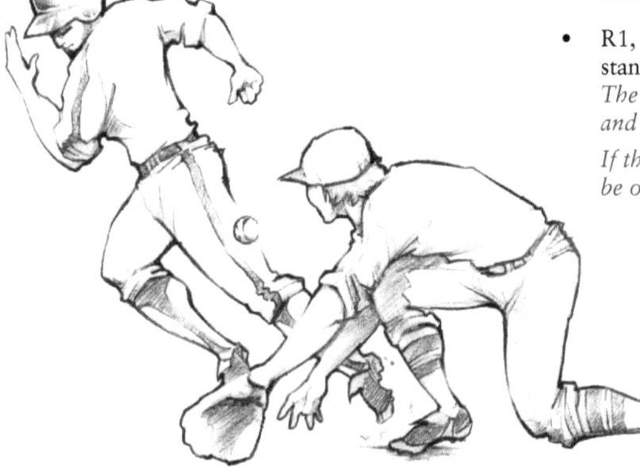

Key Points:

- If the ball touches a runner, the runner is out and the BR gets 1B. Other runners only advance if forced.
- If the ball touches an umpire, the ball is dead, the BR gets 1B. Other runners only advance if forced.
- The base is not a safe haven. A runner contacted by a fair ball on the base is out unless the infield fly rule is in effect.
- If the ball touches a fielder and then a runner, the runner is safe unless the contact was intentional.

Sample Plays:

- R1, R3, 1 out. Ground ball hits R1 between 1B and 2B.
  The ball is dead, R1 is out, R3 stays at third, the BR gets 1B.
- R2. Ground ball hit to F6. Ball goes through his legs and hits R2 directly behind the fielder. No other fielders had a chance to make a play.
  R2 is not out and the ball is in play if the contact was not intentional.
- R3. Ground ball hits the umpire stationed in the middle of the infield before it hits another fielder
  The ball is dead, R3 stays at 3B and the BR gets 1B.
- R2. Ground ball hits off F1's glove and hits the runner.
  The ball is in play unless the contact is intentional.
- R1, R2. Ground ball hits R2 who is standing on 2B.
  The ball is dead, R2 is out, the BR gets 1B and R1 advances due to being forced.

  If the ball was an infield fly, R2 would not be out, but the BR would be.

Rule 6.01(a)(10):
Interference with Fielder Fielding Batted Ball

It is interference by a batter or a runner when –

(10) He fails to avoid a fielder who is attempting to field a batted ball, or intentionally interferes with a thrown ball, provided that if two or more fielders attempt to field a batted ball, and the runner comes in contact with one or more of them, the umpire shall determine which fielder is entitled to the benefit of this rule, and shall not declare the runner out for coming in contact with a fielder other than the one the umpire determines to be entitled to field such a ball;

Key Points:

- The ball is dead and the runner is out and other runners return to the base occupied at the time of pitch.
- The fielder is protected from contact from the runner when trying to make his play. This protection extends from the fielder's initial movements to field the ball, through the act of fielding and to the act of throwing the ball. A runner who runs out of the baseline to avoid such fielder is not out.
- If the fielder misplays the ball and has to move more than a step and a reach away from his original position, he loses his protection. Any contact at this point could be ruled obstruction.
- If the ball is deflected and another fielder has a play, this second fielder is protected. This is different from a runner being contacted by a deflected batted ball (See Page #54).
- If the interference is judged to be a deliberate act to prevent a double play, then both the runner and the batter will be called out.

Sample Plays:

- R1, 1 out. B1 hits a ground ball towards F4. R1 collides with F4 while he is making his initial attempt to field the ball.
  R1 is out and the BR is put on 1B unless the interference was intentional and an obvious attempt to prevent a double play. In this case, the BR is out as well.
- B1 hits a pop-up over the 1B foul line. While running to 1B, he collides with F3 who is attempting to make the catch.
  The BR is out.
- Bases loaded. The ball is hit towards F6 and R2 hinders F6's ability to field the ball.
  R2 is out, R3 goes back to 3B, the BR is put on 1B and R1 is forced to 2B.
- R1. B1 hits the ball to F4. He misplays the ball, takes three steps while chasing the ball and collides with R1.
  R1 is not out on this play. F4 is guilty of obstruction.

Rules 5.09(a)(13) and 6.01(a)(5-7):
Willful Interference

5.09(a)

A batter is out when –

(13) A preceding runner shall, in the umpire's judgment, intentionally interfere with a fielder who is attempting to catch a thrown ball or to throw a ball in an attempt to complete any play.

6.01(a)

It is interference by a batter or a runner when –

(5) Any batter or runner who has just been put out, or any runner who has just scored, hinders or impedes any following play being made on a runner. Such runner shall be declared out for the interference of his teammate;

(6) If, in the judgment of the umpire, a base runner willfully and deliberately interferes with a batted ball or a fielder in the act of fielding a batted ball with the obvious intent to break up a double play, the ball is dead. The umpire shall call the runner out for interference and also call out the batter-runner because of the action of his teammate. In no event may bases be run or runs scored because of such action by a runner.

6.01(a)(7) is very similar to 6.01(a)(6) but covers willful and deliberate interference by a BR. In this instance, the BR is out along with the runner on base closest to home regardless of where the play might have occurred.

Sample Plays:

- R1, 1 out. B1 hits a ground ball to F6. R1 slides out of the baseline crashing into F4 as he pivots to turn the double play.
  If R1 cannot reach the base on his slide, or he hits F4 before the ground, this is interference. The ball is dead and the BR is also out.
- R1, R2, 1 out. B1 hits a ground ball to F6 that will be an easy double play. R2 slows up and lets the ball hit him.
  If judged to be willful and deliberate interference, the umpire will call R2 and the BR out and return R1 to 1B.
- R2, 1 out. R2 steals on the pitch and B1 hits a pop-up to F6. Knowing he cannot get back to 2B in time, R2 interferes with F6.
  The umpire will call both R2 and the BR out.

Definitions of Terms - INTERFERENCE and Rule 6.01(a) PENALTY:

Placing Runners After Offensive Interference

INTERFERENCE

Offensive interference is an act by the team at bat which interferes with, obstructs, impedes, hinders or confuses any fielder attempting to make a play.

6.01(a) PENALTY

The runner is out and the ball is dead if the umpire declares the batter, batter-runner, or a runner out for interference, all other runners shall return to the last base that was in the judgment of the umpire, legally touched at the time of the interference, unless otherwise provided by these rules.

In the event the batter-runner has not reached first base, all runners shall return to the base last occupied at the time of the pitch; provided, however, if during an intervening play at the plate with less than two outs a runner scores, and then the batter-runner is called out for interference outside the three-foot lane, the runner is safe and the run shall count.

Sample Plays:

- R1 is stealing on the play. B1 hits a slow roller down the 1B line. As R1 rounds 2B, the BR slaps the ball out of F3's glove.
  R1 is placed back at 1B since the BR was called out for interference before he reached 1B.
- R3, R2. R3 is in a run-down between 3B and HP. R2 advances and is touching 3B as R3 slaps the ball out of F2's glove.
  R2 is returned to 2B. He did not legally occupy 3B at the time of the interference since it still belonged to R3.
- Bases loaded, 0 outs. B1 hits a ball to F6, who throws to F4 to start a double play. R1 interferes with the pivot man.
  The BR is ruled out for R1's interference. R3 is returned to 3B. R2 is returned to 2B.

Rule 6.01(a)(8):
Physically Assisting a Base Runner

It is interference by a batter or a runner when –

> (8) In the judgment of the umpire, the base coach at third base, or first base, by touching or holding the runner, physically assists him in returning to or leaving third base or first base.

Key Points:

- This provision only stops a coach from assisting a runner. Another runner on base can help if needed.
- The rule says "physically assisting" and not touching. Giving a player a high five does not mean that player is out.
- The ball remains alive to give the defense a chance to obtain other outs.
- All other action (outs made by defense or advancement by other runners) on the play stands.

Sample Plays:

- Bases loaded, 1 out. B1 hits a ball into the gap. R3 is standing on 3B waiting to see if ball is caught. The coach comes over and pushes R3 off the base. R3, R2 and R1 all score.
  R3 is out as soon as the coach assists him. The other runs are permitted to score and the BR is allowed to stay at the base he reaches during the play.
- R2, 1 out. B1 hits a ball to F8. R2 trips rounding 3B and is helped back to the base by his coach. The BR is thrown out at 2B trying to get a double.
  R2 is out when he was assisted. Since the ball is still alive, the BR is still out at 2B.

Rule 6.01(i):
HP Collisions

(1) A runner attempting to score may not deviate from his direct pathway to the plate in order to initiate contact with the catcher (or other player covering home plate), or otherwise initiate an avoidable collision. If, in the judgment of the umpire, a runner attempting to score initiates contact with the catcher (or other player covering home plate) in such a manner, the umpire shall declare the runner out (regardless of whether the player covering home plate maintains possession of the ball). In such circumstances, the umpire shall call the ball dead, and all other base runners shall return to the last base touched at the time of the collision.

(2) Unless the catcher is in possession of the ball, the catcher cannot block the pathway of the runner as he is attempting to score. If, in the judgment of the umpire, the catcher without possession of the ball blocks the pathway of the runner, the umpire shall call or signal the runner safe. Not withstanding the above, it shall not be considered a violation of this Rule 6.01(i)(2) if the catcher blocks the pathway of the runner in a legitimate attempt to field a throw, (e.g., in reaction to the direction , trajectory, or the hop of the incoming throw, or in reaction to a throw that originates from a pitcher or drawn-in infielder).

Key Points:

- A runner will be called out (not ejected) if he contacts a player covering home plate out of the basepath without trying to score.
- A catcher is not allowed to block the plate unless he has the ball or is in the baseline in the act of fielding a throw.
- Many amateur leagues eject players for maliciously contacting a catcher. Check league rules where applicable.

Sample Plays:

- R2, 2 outs. B1 singles to F8. R2 is heading towards HP. The catcher moves in front of the plate, blocks R2, then catches the ball and tags him out.
  R2 is safe. F2 cannot block HP without the ball.
- R3 is attempting to score on a fly ball to F7. The throw beats R3 home. F2 catches the ball and is standing in front of the plate. R3 has a hard collision with F2 and the ball drops.
  R3 is safe. R3 made an effort to touch HP. R2 was blocking the plate with the ball. Both players were legal so the result of the play stands.

Rule 5.06(b)(4)(G):
Ball Thrown Out of Play

Each runner including the batter-runner may, without liability to be put out, advance –

(G) Two bases when, with no spectators on the playing field, a thrown ball goes into the stands, or into a bench (whether or not the ball rebounds into the field), or over or under or through a field fence, or on a slanting part of the screen above the backstop, or remains in the meshes of a wire screen protecting spectators. The ball is dead. When such wild throw is the first play by an infielder, the umpire, in awarding such bases, shall be governed by the position of the runners at the time the ball was pitched; in all other cases the umpire shall be governed by the position of the runners at the time the wild throw was made;

Key Points:

- Which direction a runner is going has no effect on the award. A runner returning to 1B when the ball is thrown out of play is awarded 3B.
- Neither a fake throw nor the catching of a batted ball are considered a "play" for the sake of this rule.
- The time of throw is when the ball leaves the fielder's hand and not when throw hits the ground or goes into dead ball territory.
- If the BR has not reached 1B, the award for all runners is two bases from time of pitch on the first play by an infielder.
- A pitch or a throw by F1 from the rubber that goes out of play affords the runner a one base award (5.06(b)(4)(H)).
- If the first throw from an infielder goes into the stands or dugout and the batter did not become a runner, the award is 2 bases from the time of the throw.

Sample Plays:

- R1 is running as B1 hits a sharp ball to F9 who tries to throw the BR out at 1B. The throw goes into the dugout. R1 touched 2B before the ball left F9's hand.
  Since R1 had touched 2B, he is awarded home. If the BR had reached 1B, then he is awarded 3B, otherwise he is awarded 2B.
- R1. B1 hits a shallow fly ball to F8 that drops. F8 tries to throw ball to 2B and the ball caroms out of play. At the time of throw, R1 and the BR are both between 1B and 2B.
  When two runners would be awarded the same base, place the lead runner first. In this situation, both runners will not get their full award. R1 is awarded 3B and the BR is awarded 2B.

Rule 5.06(c)(7):
Ball Lodged in Player or Umpire Equipment

The ball becomes dead and runners advance one base, or return to their bases, without liability to be put out, when –

(7) A pitched ball lodges in the umpire's or catcher's mask or paraphernalia, and remains out of play, runners advance one base;

Rule 5.06(c)(7) Comment: If a pitched ball lodges in the umpire's or catcher's mask or paraphernalia, and remains out of play, on the third strike or fourth ball, then the batter is entitled to first base and all runners advance one base. If the count on the batter is less than three balls, runners advance one base.

Key Points:

- The rules don't formally cover a batted or other thrown ball getting stuck in a player or coach's uniform. Common sense is used to place the runners in a way that nullifies the action.
- A ball that becomes lodged in a glove is considered alive and in play.

Sample Plays:

- With no one on base, B1 hits a ball that becomes stuck in F4's uniform.
  The umpire will use his judgment to place the BR – most likely at 1B.
- B1 hits a sharp ground ball to F1. The ball becomes stuck in F1's glove. He throws the entire glove to F3 who catches it before the BR reaches 1B.
  The BR is out.

Rule 5.06(b)(4)(A,F,G,H):
Ball Deflected Out of Play

Each runner including the batter-runner may, without liability to be put out, advance –

- 4 bases from time of pitch
  - Ball is deflected out of the park over fair territory while remaining in flight (5.06(b)(4)(A))
- 2 bases from time of pitch
  - Batted ball is deflected out of park over foul territory while in flight (5.06(b)(4)(F))
  - Pitch is unintentionally deflected by the catcher out of play (regardless of whether ball would have made it without being kicked (5.06(b)(4)(H) Approved Ruling)
  - Batted ball not in flight deflected off player out of play (5.06(b)(4)(F))
  - Thrown ball deflects out of play if infielder's first play (and all runners including the BR have not advanced a base) (5.06(b)(4)(G))
- 2 bases from time of throw (or deflection)
  - Pitch is intentionally deflected into the stands by the catcher or fielder (5.06(b)(4)(G)).
  - A fielder acquires possession of a ball and subsequently deflects, kicks or drops the ball out of play (5.06(b)(4)(G))
  - Thrown ball deflects out of play when thrown by an outfielder or not the first play by infielder (or first play by an infielder when all runners including the BR have advanced at least one base) (5.06(b)(4)(G) Approved Ruling)
- 1 base from time of pitch
  - Pitched ball deflects off catcher and goes into dead ball territory 5.06(b)(4)(H)

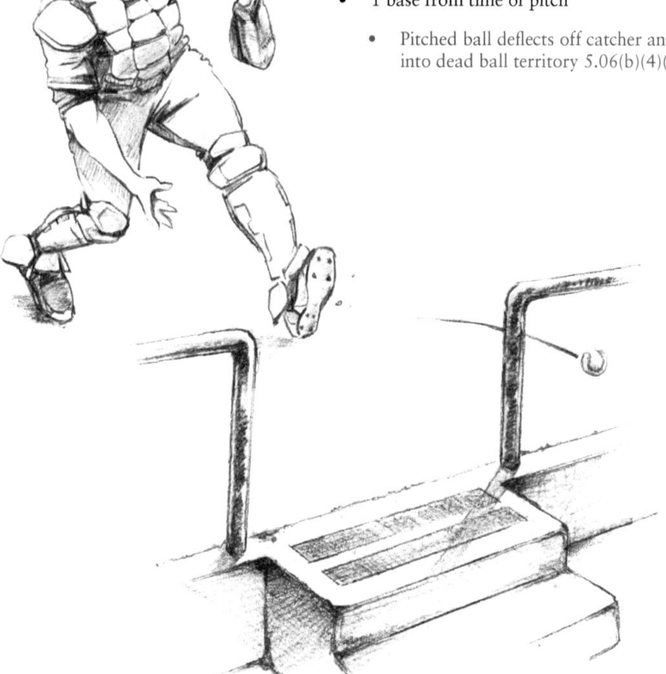

Definitions of Terms - OBSTRUCTION and Rule 6.01(h)(1):
Type 1 Obstruction

OBSTRUCTION is the act of a fielder who, while not in possession of the ball and not in the act of fielding the ball, impedes the progress of any runner.

6.01(h)

When obstruction occurs, the umpire shall call or signal "Obstruction."

(1) If a play is being made on the obstructed runner, or if the batter-runner is obstructed before he touches first base, the ball is dead and all runners shall advance, without liability to be put out, to the bases they would have reached, in the umpire's judgment, if there had been no obstruction. The obstructed runner shall be awarded at least one base beyond the base he had last legally touched before the obstruction. Any preceding runners, forced to advance by the award of bases as the penalty for obstruction, shall advance without liability to be put out.

Key Points:

- There are two types of obstruction – Type 1 is when a play is being made on the runner (See Page #64 for Type 2 Obstruction).
- A play is being made when the ball, fielder and runner are all in the same area. The BR being obstructed before 1B on a ground ball is considered Type 1 obstruction.
- A fielder who is in the immediate act of fielding a thrown ball is considered to be possession of the ball and can be in the baseline.
- The ball is immediately dead for Type 1 obstruction, except when the BR is obstructed before reaching 1B on a fly ball. In this exception, if the ball is caught, the BR is out and the ball remains alive.
- Under Type 1 obstruction, the obstructed runner must be awarded at least one base.

Sample Plays:

- R1 is in a run-down between 1B and 2B. F3 is in the baseline after throwing the ball and collides with the runner who is returning to 1B.
  Since F3 did not have the ball and a play was being made on R1, this is Type 1 obstruction. The runner is awarded a minimum of one base and placed on 2B.
- R2. B1 singles to center. F8 fields the ball and throws home in an attempt to retire R2. F2 is blocking the plate well before having the ball or while being in the act of fielding the throw. R2 never touches the plate and is tagged out.
  F2 committed obstruction and R2 will be awarded home.

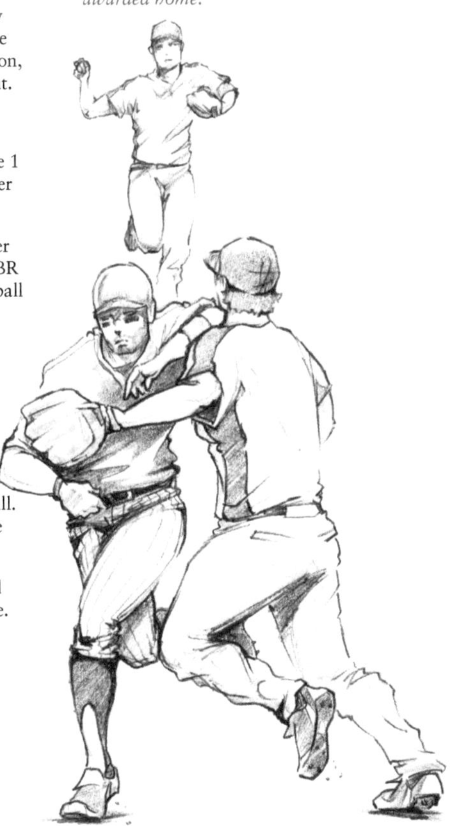

Definitions of Terms - OBSTRUCTION and Rule 6.01(h)(2):

Type 2 Obstruction

OBSTRUCTION is the act of a fielder who, while not in possession of the ball and not in the act of fielding the ball, impedes the progress of any runner.

6.01(h)(2)

When obstruction occurs, the umpire shall call or signal "Obstruction."

(2) If no play is being made on the obstructed runner, the play shall proceed until no further action is possible. The umpire shall then call "Time" and impose such penalties, if any, as in his judgment will nullify the act of obstruction.

Rule 6.01(h)(2) Comment: Under 6.01(h)(2) when the ball is not dead on obstruction and an obstructed runner advances beyond the base which, in the umpire's judgment, he would have been awarded because of being obstructed, he does so at his own peril and may be tagged out. This is a judgment call.

Key Points:

- There are two types of obstruction – Type 2 is when no immediate play is being made on the runner (See Page #63 for Type 1 Obstruction).
- A fielder who is in the immediate act of fielding a thrown ball is considered to be possession of the ball and can be in the baseline.
- The ball remains alive until the end of the play or the obstructed runner is tagged "out".
- There is no minimum base award for Type 2 obstruction.
- A runner can try to advance past the base that would have been awarded due to obstruction at his own risk.

Sample Plays:

- B1 hits a ball into the right center field gap. He collides with F3 rounding 1B and has to go back to 1B.
  The umpire will call obstruction and place the BR where he thinks he would have reached (2B or 3B) without the obstruction.
- R2. B1 hits a hard grounder past a diving F5. R2 holds up to be sure the ball gets through to the outfield. As R2 is advancing toward 3B, he collides with F5 who is getting up off the ground, but R2 reaches 3B safely. F7 fields the ground ball cleanly.
  This is Type 2 obstruction. The obstruction is ignored if the umpire judges that R2 would have stopped at 3B even without the obstruction.

Rule 6.01(e):
Spectator Interference

When there is spectator interference with any thrown or batted ball, the ball shall be dead at the moment of interference and the umpire shall impose such penalties as in his opinion will nullify the act of interference.

APPROVED RULING: If spectator interference clearly prevents a fielder from catching a fly ball, the umpire shall declare the batter out.

Key Points:

- Spectator interference means a spectator reached into or over the field to touch a ball or interfere with a fielder. A player who is prevented from making a play while reaching into the stands is not protected from spectator interference.
- The umpires have the right to use their judgment to rule on the ultimate outcome of the play. The umpires may award bases and declare outs.
- Spectator interference may be intentional or unintentional (unlike "interference by persons authorized to be on the field," which must be intentional).

Sample Plays:

- B1 hits a ball towards the outfield wall. A fan reaches over the wall and brings the ball into the stands.
  This is spectator interference, the ball is dead, and it is not a homerun. The umpire will place the BR (usually at 2B or 3B) depending on his speed, depth of the hit, and other factors.
- R3, 1 out. B1 hits a long fly ball to F9. He is camped under the ball when a fan reaches over and catches the ball.
  B1 is ruled out for spectator interference. The ball is dead immediately. The umpire scores R3 if he judges he would have scored on the sacrifice fly (a likely outcome in this play).

Rule 5.06(c)(2):
Umpire Interference

The ball becomes dead and runners advance one base, or return to their bases, without liability to be put out, when –

(2) The plate umpire interferes with the catcher's throw attempting to prevent a stolen base or retire a runner on a pick-off play; runners may not advance.

NOTE: The interference shall be disregarded if the catcher's throw retires the runner.

Rule 5.06(c)(2) Comment: Umpire interference may also occur when an umpire interferes with a catcher returning the ball to the pitcher.

Sample Plays:

- R1 is stealing on the pitch. F2 cocks his arm back to throw and hits the umpire in the mask. R1 is safe.
  The ball is dead and R1 is placed back at 1B.
- R1, R3, 1 out. R1 steals on the play. F2's arm hits the umpire as he throws. After the throw is released R3 starts towards HP. The ball arrives in time to put R1 out. R3 scores.
  The run counts. Once R1 is thrown out, the umpire interference is disregarded.
- R1, 1 out. B1 hits a ground ball off the glove of F1. Ball ricochets off the umpire.
  This type of umpire interference is governed by the rules of a batted ball hitting an umpire (See Page #54). Since the ball deflected off F1, the ball remains in play.

RULE	PAGE
3.02	13
3.03	11
3.04	12
3.05	12
3.06	12
3.07	12
4.03(a)	25
4.03(b)	25
5.04(b)(5)	38, 39, 40
5.05(a)(2)	46
5.05(b)(2)	41
5.05(b)(3)	43
5.06(a)(1)	49
5.06(a)(2)	49
5.06(b)(1)	9
5.06(b)(2)	49
5.06(b)(3)(D)	43
5.06(b)(4)(A)	33, 62
5.06(b)(4)(B)	33
5.06(b)(4)(C)	33
5.06(b)(4)(D)	33
5.06(b)(4)(E)	33
5.06(b)(4)(F)	62
5.06(b)(4)(G)	60, 62
5.06(b)(4)(H)	60, 62
5.06(b)(4)(I)	9
5.06(c)(1)	41
5.06(c)(2)	66
5.06(c)(5)	9
5.06(c)(6)	54
5.06(c)(7)	61
5.07(a)(1)	18
5.07(a)(2)	19
5.08	8
5.09(a)(1)	28
5.09(a)(2)	46

RULE	PAGE
5.09(a)(3)	46
5.09(a)(7)	39
5.09(a)(8)	40
5.09(a)(9)	40
5.09(a)(11)	45
5.09(a)(12)	31, 32
5.09(a)(13)	56
5.09(b)(1)	52
5.09(b)(2)	8, 44, 53
5.09(b)(6)	31
5.09(b)(7)	54
5.09(b)(9)	50
5.09(b)(11)	44
5.09(c)	34
5.09(c)(2)	9, 51
5.09(d)	53
5.10	16, 25
5.10(l)	26
5.11	47
6.01(a)(5)	56
6.01(a)(6)	56
6.01(a)(7)	56
6.01(a)(8)	58
6.01(a)(10)	55
6.01(a) PENALTY	45, 57
6.01(e)	65
6.01(g)	43
6.01(h)(1)	63
6.01(h)(2)	64
6.01(i)	59
6.02(a)	22,23
6.02(c)(1)	24
6.02(c)(7)	11
6.03(a)(1)	38
6.03(a)(3)	42
6.03(a)(4)	13

RULE	*PAGE*
6.03(b)(1)	36
6.03(b)(2)	36
6.03(b)(3)	36
7.01	14
7.02	14
7.03	15
Definitions of Terms - BALK	21
Definitions of Terms - CATCH	28
Definitions of Terms - FAIR BALL	37
Definitions of Terms - FORCE PLAY	30
Definitions of Terms - FOUL BALL	37
Definitions of Terms - FOUL TIP	10
Definitions of Terms - INFIELD FLY	31, 32
Definitions of Terms - INTERFERENCE	57
Definitions of Terms - OBSTRUCTION	63, 64
Definitions of Terms - STRIKE	41
Definitions of Terms - STRIKE ZONE	20
Definitions of Terms - TAG	29
Definitions of Terms - TOUCH	41

RuleGraphics Page	*Topic*	*Pre 2015 Format*	*2015 Format*
8	Scoring a Run	4.09	5.08
9	Advancing and Touching Bases	7.02, 7.05(i) Comment, 7.10(b)	5.06(b)(1),5.06(b)(4)(I) Comment, 5.09(c)(2)
10	Foul Tip	2.00 FOUL TIP	Definitions of Terms - FOUL TIP
11	Uniforms	1.11, 8.02(b)	3.03, 6.02(c)(7)
12	Glove Specifications	1.12, 1.13, 1.14 and 1.15	3.04, 3.05, 3.06, 3.07
13	Bats	1.10, 6.06(d)	3.02,6.03(a)(4)
14	Called or Suspended Games	4.10, 4.12	7.01, 7.02
15	Forfeits	4.15, 4.16, 4.17	7.03
16	Substituting	3.03	5.10
18'	The Windup Position	8.01(a)	5.07(a)(1)
19	The Set Position	8.01(b)	5.07(a)(2)
20	Strike Zone	2.00 STRIKE ZONE	Definitions of Terms - STRIKE ZONE
21	Balk - Basic Definition	2.00 BALK, 8.05 PENALTY	Definitions of Terms - BALK, 6.02(a) PENALTY
22	Step Balk	8.05(b)(c)	6.02(a)(2-3)
23	Other Balks	8.05	6.02(a)
24	Pitcher Going to his Mouth	8.02(a)(1)	6.02(c)(1)
25	Substituting for the Pitcher	3.05	5.10
26	Pitcher/Manager Visits	8.06	5.10(l)
28	Catch	2.00 CATCH, 6.05(a)	Definitions of Terms - CATCH, 5.09(a)(1)
29	Tag Plays (Base and Player)	2.00 TAG	Definitions of Terms - TAG
30	Force Play	2.00 FORCE PLAY	Defintions of Terms - FORCE PLAY
31	Infield Fly Rule	2.00 INFIELD FLY	Definition of Terms - INFIELD FLY
32	Infielder Intentionally Dropping Batted Ball	6.05(l)	5.09(a)(12)
33	Detached Player Equipment	7.05(a)(b)(c)(d)(e)	5.06(b)(4)(A-E)
34	Appeal Plays	7.10	5.09(c)
36	Batting Out of Order	6.07(a)(b)	6.03(b)(1-3)
37	Fair/Foul Ball	2.00 FAIR BALL, 2.00 FOUL BALL	Definitions of Terms - FAIR BALL, FOUL BALL
38	Batter's Box	6.03, 6.06(a)	5.04(b)(5), 6.03(a)(1)
39	Batted Ball Hits Batter	6.05(g), 6.03	5.09(a)(7), 5.04(b)(5)

RuleGraphics Page	*Topic*	*Pre 2015 Format*	*2015 Format*
40	Bat Infractions around HP	6.05(h), 6.03	5.09(a)(8), 5.04(b)(5)
41	Hit by Pitch	6.08(b)	5.05(b)(2)
42	Batter Interference with Catcher	6.06(c)	6.03(a)(3)
43	Catcher's Interference	6.08(c)	5.05(b)(3)
44	Overrunning First Base	7.08(j)	5.09(b)(11)
45	Runner's Lane Interference	6.05(k)	5.09(a)(11)
46	Uncaught Third Strike	6.05(b)(c), 6.09(b)	5.09(a)(2-3),5.05(a)(2)
47	Designated Hitter	6.10(b)	5.11
49	Two Runners Occupying a Base	7.01, 7.03	5.06(a)(1-2),5.06(b)(2)
50	Passing Another Runner on the Bases	7.08(h)	5.09(b)(9)
51	Retouching Bases When Ball is Dead	7.10(b)	5.09(c)(2)
52	Runner Out of Baseline	7.08(a)(1)	5.09(b)(1)
53	Abandoning Base Paths	7.08(a)(2)	5.09(b)(2)
54	Runner/Umpire Hit by Batted Ball	5.09(f), 7.08(f)	5.06(c)(6), 5.09(b)(7)
55	Interference with Fielder Fielding Batted Ball	7.09(j)	6.01(a)(10)
56	Willful Interference	6.05(m), 7.09(e)(f)(g)	5.09(a)(13),6.01(a)(5-7)
57	Placing Runners After Offensive Interference	2.00 INTERFERENCE	Definitions of Terms - INTERFERENCE, 6.01(a) PENALTY
58	Physically Assisting a Base Runner	7.09(h)	6.01(a)(8)
59	HP Collisions	7.13	6.01(i)
60	Ball Thrown Out of Play	7.05(g)	5.06(b)(4)(G)
61	Ball Lodged in Player or Umpire Equipment	5.09(g)	5.06(c)(7)
62	Ball Deflected Out of Play	7.05(a)(f)(g)(h)	5.06(b)(4)(A,F,G,H)
63	Type 1 Obstruction	2.00 OBSTRUCTION, 7.06(a)	Definitions of Terms - OBSTRUCTION, 6.01(h)(1)
64	Type 2 Obstruction	2.00 OBSTRUCTION, 7.06(b)	Definitions of Terms - OBSTRUCTION, 6.01(h)(2)
65	Spectator Interference	3.16	6.01(e)
66	Umpire Interference	5.09(b)	5.06(c)(2)

RuleGraphics Page	Topic	OBR Rule(s)	High School Rule(s)	Major Differences
8	Scoring a Run	5.08	9-1-1	None
9	Advancing and Touching Bases	5.06(b)(1),5.06(b)(4)(I) Comment, 5.09(c)(2)	8-2-1, 8-2-2, 8-2-3 NOTE, 8-2-6(d), 8-2-9	* A base runner on or beyond a base past a missed or not tagged up base when the ball becomes dead is subject to being out on appeal
10	Foul Tip	Definitions of Terms - FOUL TIP	2-16-2	None
11	Uniforms	3.03, 6.02(c)(7)	1-4-1, 1-4-2, 1-4-3	* Umpires can remove anyting deemed distracting * No jewelry except taped down religious and/or medical jewelry * Helmets always required while on live ball territory while ball is live * Catcher's headgear must cover ears
12	Glove Specifications	3.04, 3.05, 3.06, 3.07	1-3-6, 1-5-7	* Any fielder can wear a 1st basemen's glove * Penalty for touching fair ball with illegal glove is 3 bases
13	Bats	3.02,6.03(a)(4)	1-3-2, 1-3-3, 1-3-5	* Bats can be non-wood * Non-wood bats must adhere to BBCOR standards and have label permanently affixed * Bats can be no longer than 36 inches and cannot weight more than 3 ozs less than length * Batter is out and coach is restricted after illegal bat is used - coach ejected after second offense
14	Called or Suspended Games	7.01, 7.02	4-2-1, 4-2-2, 4-2-3, 4-2-4	* Games are seven innings * A complete game is five innings (or 4 1/2 if home team ahead) * Games can be shortened due to run rules (by state association adoption)
15	Forfeits	7.03	4-4-1(f)	* A team can finish a game with 8 players

RuleGraphics Page	Topic	OBR Rule(s)	High School Rule(s)	Major Differences
16	Substituting	5.10	3-1-1, 3-1-2, 3-1-3	* Starting players can re-enter once provided it is same spot in batting order * Unreported subs become in the game after ball becomes live * Illegal subs found on offense are declared out, if they complete an at bat the defense has until the next pitch to discover - player is out and all outs on play stand, all other runners return * If a play is made by illegal substitute on defense, offense has choice of taking or replaying the play
18	The Windup Position	5.07(a)(1)	6-1-2	* Free foot must be on or behind the line through the front edge of the rubber * Pitchers cannot attempt pick offs from the windup position
19	The Set Position	5.07(a)(2)	6-1-3	* Pivot foot has to be parallel to and completely touching rubber * Free foot must be entirely in front of rubber
20	Strike Zone	Definitions of Terms - STRIKE ZONE	2-35	* Zone is determined from batter's natural stance
21	Balk - Basic Definition	Definitions of Terms - BALK, 6.02(a) PENALTY	2-3, 5-1-1(k)	* Balks cause the ball to becomes immediately dead
22	Step Balk	6.02(a)(2-3)	6-2-4	* High school pitchers can feint to third base
23	Other Balks	6.02(a)	6-2-4, 6-2-5	* Pitcher cannot be within 5 feet of the rubber without the ball
24	Pitcher Going to his Mouth	6.02(c)(1)	6-2-1(e)	* A pitcher who goes to his mouth on the rubber has committed an illegal pitch * A pitcher who goes to his mouth while off the rubber and then engages rubber without wiping off fingers is penalized with a ball to the batter

RuleGraphics Page	Topic	OBR Rule(s)	High School Rule(s)	Major Differences
25	Substituting for the Pitcher	5.10	3-1-1 PEN, 3-1-2	* A starting pitcher who does not face a batter cannot return to the mound later in the game but they may play another position
26	Pitcher/ Manager Visits	5.10(l)	3-4-1, 3-4-3	* A manager is allocated three conferences per game. After 3, the pitcher is removed from mound for rest of game * Prior to 3 conferences, if pitcher is removed, it is not counted as a conference * Conference ends when manager crosses foul line * A meeting with any defensive player counts as a conference
28	Catch	Definitions of Terms - CATCH, 5.09(a)(1)	2-9-1, 8-4-1(b)	* A fielder can have one foot in dead ball territory and one ball in live ball territory and make a legal catch
29	Tag Plays (Base and Player)	Definitions of Terms - TAG	2-24-1, 2-24-4	* A player who loses the ball right after touching a base has performed a legal tag if he had secured the ball before the touch
30	Force Play	Defintions of Terms - FORCE PLAY	2-29-3	None
31	Infield Fly Rule	Definition of Terms - INFIELD FLY	2-19	None
32	Infielder Intentionally Dropping Batted Ball	5.09(a)(12)	8-4-1(c)	None
33	Detached Player Equipment	5.06(b)(4)(A-E)	8-3-3(a)(b)(c), 8-3-4	* A pitch touched by detached equipment is a 2 base award
34	Appeal Plays	5.09(c)	8-2-5, 8-2-6	* Any defensive player or coach can appeal during a dead ball * An offense initiated play does not cancel the defense's ability to appeal
36	Batting Out of Order	6.03(b)(1-3)	7-1-1, 7-1-2	* Any outs made on play when a batter bats out of order stand

RuleGraphics Page	Topic	OBR Rule(s)	High School Rule(s)	Major Differences
37	Fair/Foul Ball	Definitions of Terms - FAIR BALL, FOUL BALL	2-5-1, 2-16-1	* A ball that touches the ground beyond an imaginary line between first and third is a fair ball
38	Batter's Box	5.04(b)(5), 6.03(a)(1)	7-3-2, 2-7-2	* A batter whose foot is on the plate while making contact is out - even if he is still in the batter's box
39	Batted Ball Hits Batter	5.09(a)(7), 5.04(b)(5)	8-4-2(k)	* A batter is in the batter's box (for purposes of this rule) as long as one foot is still completely in the box
40	Bat Infractions around HP	5.09(a)(8), 5.04(b)(5)	8-4-1(d), 7-4-1(i), 7-3-6	None
41	Hit by Pitch	5.05(b)(2)	8-1-1(d)	None
42	Batter Interference with Catcher	6.03(a)(3)	7-3-5	* Follow-through interference is treated the same as all other batter's interference
43	Catcher's Interference	5.05(b)(3)	8-1-1(e)	* A balk is not called when the catcher interferes with a batter on a squeeze play. Runners only advance is stealing on pitch
44	Overrunning First Base	5.09(b)(11)	8-2-7, 8-4-2(p)	* A runner is in jeopardy of being put out if he overruns first base on a walk
45	Runner's Lane Interference	5.09(a)(11)	8-4-1(g)	* If the batter-runner and catcher are on the same side of the foul line, a quality throw is not needed to rule interference
46	Uncaught Third Strike	5.09(a)(2-3),5.05(a)(2)	7-4-1(b), 8-1-1(b)	* A runner unaware of his situation can still run to first as long as he has not entered the dugout (or all infielders have not left fair territory)
47	Designated Hitter	5.11	3-1-4	* A hitter can be designated for any defensive player * The DH and player being hit for are locked into their batting order spot * The DH has re-entry privileges even if the role of DH has been terminated

RuleGraphics Page	Topic	OBR Rule(s)	High School Rule(s)	Major Differences
49	Two Runners Occupying a Base	5.06(a)(1-2),5.06(b)(2)	8-2-8	None
50	Passing Another Runner on the Bases	5.09(b)(9)	8-4-2(m)	* Passing creates a time play with the exception of awarded bases. Any runner awarded home is allowed to score even if passing happens for out 3 before he scores
51	Retouching Bases When Ball is Dead	5.09(c)(2)	8-4-2(q), 8-2-5	* A runner's location when the ball becomes dead determines if he can legally re-touch. Runners on or beyond a base past the missed (or tagged up) base are subject to appeal
52	Runner Out of Baseline	5.09(b)(1)	8-4-2(a)	None
53	Abandoning Base Paths	5.09(b)(2)	8-4-2(p)	* If a game ends on an awarded base situation, all runners have to touch their next forced base or be subject to being out for abandonment
54	Runner/Umpire Hit by Batted Ball	5.06(c)(6), 5.09(b)(7)	8-4-2(k), 5-1-1(f)	* A runner hit by a ball when behind the infielders (and no other infielder has a play) is not out. The ball does not have to pass directly by or through a fielder
55	Interference with Fielder Fielding Batted Ball	6.01(a)(10)	8-4-2(g)	None
56	Willful Interference	5.09(a)(13),6.01(a)(5-7)	8-4-2(g)	* In order to call 2 outs for interference, the umpire only has to be convinced the inteference prevented a double play - not that the runner willfully interfered with the intent to stop a double play * The second runner who is out is always the runner being played on - if unsure, then the umpire will call out runner closest to home

RuleGraphics Page	Topic	OBR Rule(s)	High School Rule(s)	Major Differences
57	Placing Runners After Offensive Interference	Definitions of Terms - INTERFER-ENCE, 6.01(a) PENALTY	8-2-9, 8-4-2(b) PEN	* Runners are placed on the base they reached at the time of the interference * Exception is force play slide rule where runners are placed where they were at time of pitch
58	Physically Assisting a Base Runner	6.01(a)(8)	3-2-2	* Runners placed on last base touched at the time of the infraction
59	HP Collisions	6.01(i)	8-4-2(e),3-3-1(m)	* The runner can never maliciously crash into the catcher (even if obstructed) * The ball is dead, the runner is out (unless he scored before the collision), and the runner is ejected
60	Ball Thrown Out of Play	5.06(b)(4)(G)	8-3-3(c)(d), 8-3-5	None
61	Ball Lodged in Player or Umpire Equipment	5.06(c)(7)	8-3-3(c)(d)(f)	* A ball lodged in a player's glove or uniform is dead with a 2 base award * Ball lodged in offensive uniform allows the runner to acquire the base they were running towards
62	Ball Deflected Out of Play	5.06(b)(4) (A,F,G,H)	8-3-3(a)(c)(d)	* A ball that would have gone out of play regardless of being touched by the catcher (umpire judgement) results in a one base award from the time of pitch * A ball that would have remained in play if not defelcted in a 2 base award from the time of deflection
63	Type 1 Obstruction	Definitions of Terms - OB-STRUCTION, 6.01(h)(1)	N/A	N/A

RuleGraphics Page	Topic	OBR Rule(s)	High School Rule(s)	Major Differences
64	Type 2 Obstruction	Definitions of Terms - OBSTRUCTION, 6.01(h)(2)	2-22-1, 2-22-2, 2-22-3, 8-3-2	* All obstruction is a delayed dead ball * Play continues until all action is complete (even if obstructed runner is put out) * A minimum of one base is awarded on obstruction * A defensive player cannot block a base without the ball - even if in the act of fielding a throw
65	Spectator Interference	6.01(e)	2-21-3, 5-1-1(f)(3)	None
66	Umpire Interference	5.06(c)(2)	5-1-2(c)	None
N/A	Speed Up Rules		Pg 64	* A player who has not previously been in the game can run for the catcher or pitcher * A player cannot be a courtesy runner and a sub in the same half inning * The courtesy runner is attached to the position (either pitcher or catcher) and not the player * The coutesy runner is for the player who last played pitcher or catcher (not the one coming in the next inning, and not a pinch hitter for the previous pitcher or catcher)
N/A	Force Play Slide Rule		2-32-2, 8-4-2(b)	* On a force out, the runner must slide legally, on the ground, and in a direct line between the bases * Penalty is runner and batter-runner are out. All others return to time of pitch base

RuleGraphics Page	Topic	OBR Rule(s)	College Rule(s)	Major Differences
8	Scoring a Run	5.08	5-6-c	None
9	Advancing and Touching Bases	5.06(b)(1),5.06(b)(4)(I) Comment, 5.09(c)(2)	8-1-a,8-6-a-3 (AR-2)	None
10	Foul Tip	Definitions of Terms - FOUL TIP	2-37	None
11	Uniforms	3.03, 6.02(c)(7)	1-14,9-2-e	None
12	Glove Specifications	3.04, 3.05, 3.06, 3.07	1-13	* If play is made with illegal equipment, offensive team has choice to take result of play or have play voided or replayed
13	Bats	3.02,6.03(a)(4)	1-12,7-10-b	* Bats can be non-wood * Non-wood bats must have a certification mark on barrell signifying legality * Bats can be no longer than 36 inches and cannot weight more than 3 ozs less than length * Batter is out if he uses a bat that is tampered to improve distance. If detected before first pitch, the bat is removed
14	Called or Suspended Games	7.01, 7.02	5-8,5-9	* Seven inning games can be part of a doubleheader by conference rule or mutual agreement * A complete game is five innings (or 4 1/2 if home team ahead) * Games can be shortened due to a run rule by mutual consent or conference ruling
15	Forfeits	7.03	5-12	None

RuleGraphics Page	Topic	OBR Rule(s)	College Rule(s)	Major Differences
16	Substituting	5.10	5-5	* Illegal subs found on offense are declared out, if they complete an at bat the defense has until the next pitch to discover - all action is invalidated * If a play is made by illegal substitute on defense, offense has choice of taking or replaying the play * A pitcher can be returned to the mound once per game (if not in violation of conference rule)
18	The Windup Position	5.07(a)(1)	9-1-a	None
19	The Set Position	5.07(a)(2)	9-1-b	None
20	Strike Zone	Definitions of Terms - STRIKE ZONE	2-73	None
21	Balk - Basic Definition	Definitions of Terms - BALK, 6.02(a) PEN-ALTY	2-3,9-3-PEN	None
22	Step Balk	6.02(a)(2-3)	9-3-b,9-3-c	* College pitchers can feint to third base
23	Other Balks	6.02(a)	9-3	* Along with entire free foot, no part of stride leg can break back edge of rubber without pitcher delivering to home (or 2nd) * Pitcher cannot be on any part of dirt circle around mound without the ball
24	Pitcher Going to his Mouth	6.02(c)(1)	9-2-d	* A ball is called each time this occurs (no warning)
25	Substituting for the Pitcher	5.10	5-5-b, 9-4-f	* A starting pitcher that does not face a batter could be moved to another position or DH, but they cannot return to the mound

RuleGraphics Page	Topic	OBR Rule(s)	College Rule(s)	Major Differences
26	Pitcher/ Manager Visits	5.10(l)	9-4	* A manager is allocated three free conferences per game plus 1 for extra innings. Unused conferences can carry over * Prior to 3 conferences, if pitcher is removed, it is not counted as a conference * A meeting with any defensive player counts as a conference
28	Catch	Definitions of Terms - CATCH, 5.09(a)(1)	2-16,7-11-c	None
29	Tag Plays (Base and Player)	Definitions of Terms - TAG	2-76	None
30	Force Play	Defintions of Terms - FORCE PLAY	2-33	None
31	Infield Fly Rule	Definition of Terms - INFIELD FLY	2-48	None
32	Infielder Intentionally Dropping Batted Ball	5.09(a)(12)	7-11-q	None
33	Detached Player Equipment	5.06(b)(4)(A-E)	8-3-g,8-3-h	None
34	Appeal Plays	5.09(c)	8-6	* An offense initiated play does not cancel the defense's ability to appeal
36	Batting Out of Order	6.03(b)(1-3)	7-11-a	None
37	Fair/Foul Ball	Definitions of Terms - FAIR BALL, FOUL BALL	2-27,2-35	None
38	Batter's Box	5.04(b)(5), 6.03(a)(1)	7-1-e,7-10-a	* A batter whose foot is on the plate while making contact is out - even if he is still in the batter's box
39	Batted Ball Hits Batter	5.09(a)(7), 5.04(b)(5)	7-11-l, 7-1-e	None
40	Bat Infractions around HP	5.09(a)(8), 5.04(b)(5)	7-11-m,7-1-e	None
41	Hit by Pitch	5.05(b)(2)	8-2-d	None
42	Batter Interference with Catcher	6.03(a)(3)	7-11-f	None

RuleGraphics Page	Topic	OBR Rule(s)	College Rule(s)	Major Differences
43	Catcher's Interference	5.05(b)(3)	8-2-e, 8-3-p	None
44	Overrunning First Base	5.09(b)(11)	8-5-i Exc	None
45	Runner's Lane Interference	5.09(a)(11)	7-11-p	None
46	Uncaught Third Strike	5.09(a)(2-3),5.05(a)(2)	7-11-g, 7-11-h, 7-11-u	None
47	Designated Hitter	5.11	7-2	* In a 9 man lineup, the P/DH are the same person * When P/DH are same person, the person can stay in one role even if taken out from the other * If P and DH are separate players, if one is taken out, they can take the other role * DH role not lost if person DH-ing bats for the P * Hardest rule in book - many other facets to this
49	Two Runners Occupying a Base	5.06(a)(1-2),5.06(b)(2)	8-1-c, 8-3-a	None
50	Passing Another Runner on the Bases	5.09(b)(9)	8-5-m	None
51	Retouching Bases When Ball is Dead	5.09(c)(2)	8-6-a-3 (AR-2)	None
52	Runner Out of Baseline	5.09(b)(1)	8-5-a	None
53	Abandoning Base Paths	5.09(b)(2)	8-5-c	* If a game ends on an awarded base situation, all runners have to touch their next forced base or be subject to being out for abandonment
54	Runner/Umpire Hit by Batted Ball	5.06(c)(6), 5.09(b)(7)	8-2-f, 8-5-k	* A runner hit by a ball when behind all infielders who had a chance to make the play is not out. The ball does not have to pass directly by or through a fielder
55	Interference with Fielder Fielding Batted Ball	6.01(a)(10)	8-5-d	None

RuleGraphics Page	Topic	OBR Rule(s)	College Rule(s)	Major Differences
56	Willful Interference	5.09(a)(13),6.01(a)(5-7)	7-11-r, 8-5-d, 8-5-e	None
57	Placing Runners After Offensive Interference	Definitions of Terms - INTERFERENCE, 6.01(a) PENALTY	2-51	* Runners are placed on the base they legally reached at the time of the interference unless there is an intervening play * Exception is force play slide rule where runners are placed where they were at time of pitch
58	Physically Assisting a Base Runner	6.01(a)(8)	8-5-f, 3-3-e	None
59	HP Collisions	6.01(i)	8-7	* The runner has to make an attempt to reach the base * The runner may not attempt to dislodge the ball (contact above waist is considered an attempt) * The runner must avoid a collision if he can reach base without colliding * If the catcher has control of ball, is blocking the plate, and the three conditions above or met, the play is called an unavoidable collision * Otherwise, penalize the catcher if he does not have the ball or the runner if he violates one of the three conditions
60	Ball Thrown Out of Play	5.06(b)(4)(G)	8-3-o-3	None
61	Ball Lodged in Player or Umpire Equipment	5.06(c)(7)	8-3-k, 8-3-l	None
62	Ball Deflected Out of Play	5.06(b)(4)(A,F,G,H)	8-3-o-2, 8-3-o-3, 8-3-o-4, 8-3-o-4 (AR-1), 6-4-d	None
63	Type 1 Obstruction	Definitions of Terms - OBSTRUCTION, 6.01(h)(1)	2-55, 8-3-e-1	* A player fielding a pickoff throw must clearly have possession of ball before blocking base

RuleGraphics Page	Topic	OBR Rule(s)	College Rule(s)	Major Differences
64	Type 2 Obstruction	Definitions of Terms - OB-STRUCTION, 6.01(h)(2)	2-55, 8-3-e-2	None
65	Spectator Interference	6.01(e)	7-11-t, 8-3-n	None
66	Umpire Interference	5.06(c)(2)	6-3-a	None
N/A	Force Play Slide Rule		8-4	* On any force play, if the runner slides, it either has to be away from contact or in a direct line between the two bases * If he does not slide, the runner must veer away from the fielder * Contact can occur on top of or past the base * Whether the defense could complete the play has no bearing on the decision * Penalty is runner and batter-runner are out. All other return to time of pitch base

Acknowledgements

First and foremost, I would like to thank the Office of the Commissioner of Major League Baseball for allowing me to use the Official Baseball Rules for this project.

It takes a lot of work to make something complex very simple. As such, lots of people have influenced and helped along the way. If I miss anyone, I apologize – I did not have the benefit of instant replay when making the list.

- Kara– Thanks for being an umpire widow for spring/summer weekends with no complaints. Thank for your steady hand of support in this project no matter how far away it sounded. Sharing life with you continues to be the best call I ever made
- Evan and Alex – Two of the most promising umpires I know. Thanks for letting dad indulge in his hobby
- Gene and Debby – Thanks for giving me a good attention to detail, a strong work ethic, and having an ear for the minutiae of umpiring without getting bored. I hope to show the same level of interest in my children's hobbies
- John and Connie – Thanks for consistently and selflessly lending a hand when I am out working
- Andrew – Helped guide the project from day 1. Hopefully the first of many
- Alan and Sean – You both constantly amazed me with the quality of design and art. This project is infinitely better than I first imagined due to your contributions
- Bob – Thanks for your efforts in editing. Your work added validity and confidence to the final product
- Damien – Thanks for the quick look at the introduction section. More broadly thanks for being the starting point for many creative outlets
- Greg – Between broken bulletin boards and endless fungos, you gave me my first job in umpiring. I appreciate the support in this and other endeavors over the years
- Randall – Thanks for your help in legal portions of the project
- Indianapolis Umpires Association – The effort and dedication they put into training umpires is unmatched. I cannot imagine working for a better association.
- Partners too numerous to mention – I appreciate all the pre and post-game rule discussions in parking lots

The Writer: Dennis Goodman

Unable to hit a curve ball, Dennis started umpiring youth baseball in 1994. He has umpired state tournaments at the high school and youth level. In 2013 he joined the Indianapolis Umpires Association (IUA). He has been a member of the Society for American Baseball Research (SABR) since 2002. He lives outside Indianapolis with his wife and two sons.

The Illustrator: Sean Perdue

Sean is a Nashville based artist specializing in various mediums while concentrating his skills in the home building industry. He creates his own unique pieces and works on joint projects in the collaborative studio as a member of Noble Building Group.

For more, go to **www.noblebuildinggroup.com.**

The Designer: Alan Knight

Alan is president and creative director at Creative Roots Design Group, based in Indianapolis, where he lives with his wife and son.

To see some of their other work, check out **www.creativerootsdg.com.**

CPSIA information can be obtained
at www.ICGtesting.com
Printed in the USA
BVHW02n1149040418
512043BV00001BA/27/P